Millions of men and women silently carry the grief of a secret abortion in their hearts. They are silenced by shame. They are silenced by the belief that they are alone and no one can understand their pain. Indeed, they fear that "it's just something wrong with me. No one else feels this way after an abortion."

These walking wounded need to learn that we do understand. They need to know that it is normal and necessary not only to grieve after an abortion, but also to seek emotional and spiritual healing. It is our obligation, as Christians, to help them escape their feelings of shame and to find peace in God's forgiveness.

Dr. David C. Reardon, Director of the Elliot Institute[1]

1 *Quote from "The Jericho Plan: Breaking Down the Walls Which Prevent Post-Abortion Healing" by Dr. David C. Reardon, Director of the Elliot Institute, 18-19*

DEDICATION

This book is dedicated to my husband Joel and our children, Zach and Jenna. You are the sweetest support team a girl could ever want! Thank you for believing in me, encouraging me, and sacrificing time with me during the writing of this book. And to Socrates, "Who's a good boy?!" for curling up next to me and keeping me company.

MARY COMM

SECRET SIN

WHEN GOD'S PEOPLE CHOOSE

ABORTION

UNMASKING THE SECRET SHAME &
SILENT SUFFERING OF POST-ABORTION CHRISTIANS

SECRET SIN
WHEN GODS PEOPLE CHOOSE ABORTION

ISBN: 1-60037-149-3 (Hardcover)
ISBN: 1-60037-148-5 (Paperback)

Published by:

Morgan James Publishing, LLC
1225 Franklin Ave Ste 325
Garden City, NY 11530-1693
Toll Free 800-485-4943
www.MorganJamesPublishing.com

General Editor:
Heather Campbell

Cover & Interior Design by:
3 Dog Design
www.3dogdesign.net
chris@3dogdesign.net

CONTENTS

Preface   iii

Dedication   iv

Acknowledgements   v

Introduction   vi

Chapter 1: Christian's Don't Have Abortions Do They?   1
Understanding Who Chooses Abortion and Why

Chapter 2: The Lies We Have Believed   13
Debunking the Myths about Abortion

Chapter 3: Abortion's Hold on Those it Touches   29
Common Reactions & Responses To Abortion

Chapter 4: Suffering Silently In Our Midst   37
Why Post-Abortive Christians Don't Seek Healing from Their
Abortions & How to Recognize Them

Chapter 5: Our Record/Our Wrongs – And How to Correct Them   43
How the church Has Missed the Mark and What We Can
Do to Affect Change

Chapter 6: Seeing the Post-Abortive Through God's Eyes   53

Chapter 7: Making the church a Safe Place for the Post-Abortive   63
How to Cultivate Compassion for the Post-Abortive Among
the Non-Abortive

Chapter 8: When the Touch of Abortion Embitters   71
Understanding Those Wounded by an Abortion They
Couldn't Prevent

Chapter 9: Slowing the Onslaught/Turning the Tide -   **75**
The Healing Cycle and How it Reduces the Incidence of
Abortion in America

Chapter 10: How to Begin Preparing for Abortion Recovery   **79**
in Your church
Learn the Truth; Share the Truth; Pray for God's Favor

Appendix   **87**

Resources   **89**

You Can Help Turn The Tide of Abortion   **93**

ACKNOWLEDGEMENTS

This book would not have become a reality without my biggest fans and supporters, my husband Joel and our two children, Zach and Jenna. Thank you for encouraging me, for cheering me on, and for making the sacrifice of time during the writing of this book.

Jeanenne, thank you for being such a faithful, loving, and supportive friend. Our Tuesday morning breakfasts are essential sanity breaks and a highlight of my week.

To our prayer team, Kiley, Cynthia, Ken, Stephanie, Mark J., Cheryl, Carol, Mark G., Katherine, Kristi, Shelly, and Carmen: thank you for lifting this book and this ministry to the Throne of Grace. We wouldn't be here without your faithful intercession.

David, thank you for recognizing the need for this book and for supporting me through the writing process. Thanks also to Jeanette and Heather for the great job you did on transforming this manuscript into a quality book.

To my mom and dad: thank you for loving Jesus and for teaching me to do the same. Thank you for raising me in the church and for praying for me all my life. Thank you for modeling the Christian life for me and for being the kind of parents I like spending time with. You are precious to me.

And finally, thank You, Loving Father, Gentle Shepherd, Gracious God, Holy Spirit, and Lord of my life for choosing me for Yourself. Thank You for knowing me more than any other and loving me anyway. Thank You for redeeming my life, rescuing me from my sin, and restoring me to service in this ministry. You are my All in all and my reason for being. All I do is for You.

INTRODUCTION

Although the evangelical church has worked diligently over the past three decades to save the lives of the unborn, we have yet to establish ourselves as a safe place for those that have been hurt by abortion to find hope and healing in Jesus Christ. Generally speaking, we have yet to compassionately embrace the men and women – the mothers, fathers, family members, friends, and medical personnel – whose lives have been devastated by abortion. Abortion, as with other issues in the past, is still "in the closet" where the church is concerned.

Sadly, most pastors, ministry leaders and others within the church are unaware of how abortion affects the lives of those that have survived it and how many of them are filling our pews on Sunday morning, suffering in silence under a shroud of guilt and shame. Many pastors and church leaders see the high divorce rate, the troubled marriages, depression, eating disorders, substance abuse, pornography addiction and other self-destructive behaviors plaguing their congregants, but few have recognized the deeper issue that often lies at the root of these problems: the life-altering wound left in the wake of an unresolved abortion experience - a wound that at the very least one-third of our women and an additional one-third of our men have experienced firsthand.

I was one of those women. I have not experienced an abortion firsthand, but as an accomplice to an abortion in my early twenties I have known the pain of regret and the stab of guilt knowing my dear friend took the life of her child – and that her decision was partially the result of my influence in her life. The blood of her child was upon my hands.

I suffered for years from this guilt as I watched her make one self-destructive choice after another. My heart broke for her each time she punished herself—even though she wasn't even aware that's what she was doing. Both of us were in a cycle of pain, but unaware of why. We lacked knowledge and understanding, even though the feelings of guilt, shame and regret were persistent.

I am a Christian and have been since the tender age of nine. I was raised in a Christian home by parents that were devoted servants of God. My friend was also a professing Christian. We knew God; had walked with God. And though neither of us had talked about it, had someone asked us prior to that decisive moment I have no doubt we would've proclaimed a pro-life view. We knew that abortion ended the life of an unborn child, but that knowledge wasn't enough to persuade either of us to do the right thing when the fear and panic of this ill-timed pregnancy arose.

Years later as God revealed my sin to me and as I repented with much sorrow and remorse, He gave me compassion for others that had been similarly touched by abortion. As a result I began working with people in crisis pregnancy situations as well as post-abortive pain. What I discovered was shocking: Most of those I ministered to were either Christians or significantly religious, having been raised in the church. Many knew as I did that abortion was wrong, but had made the same choice my friend and I had made.

A recent study[1] showed that the women experiencing the greatest degree of post-abortion trauma issues are pro-life and/or Christian women. This study reported that 65% of women having abortions experienced multiple post-traumatic stress disorder symptoms and women who are more likely to experience a negative reaction:

(a) Had feelings against abortion prior to the procedure
(b) Were pressured to abort
(c) Had deeply-felt religious views or
(d) Received little or no counseling prior to the abortion

In addition to the women, we have also learned that the father of the aborted baby often experiences similar symptoms of Post-Abortion Syndrome (PAS). [I will talk more about PAS later in the book.] Likewise everyone within the family is affected: the grandparents, the aunts and uncles, the siblings (both current and future), and grandchildren. Friends involved in the decision-making process will also exhibit symptoms of PAS, as well as the medical personnel that either by choice or by circumstance performed abortions.

In all my years of attending and serving in the church I have seen "the look" in countless pairs of eyes – the look that an abortion wound leaves – regardless of the smiles and laughter and devotion to God, the look remains. It is a look of soul-sickness, a deep sorrow that radiates from a heart that has been broken by a wound it was never meant to survive, much less endure. Many of them are unaware of the source of their woundedness having so convinced themselves that the choice they made was the right one, or that because God has forgiven them, all has been righted. But still the look remains. The shame keeps the secret well hidden so that most people would never even realize they're wounded. But the woundedness persists, permitting their past sin to become a stronghold that the enemy of God uses against them at every possible turn, keeping them from being effective servants of Christ. Those that should be mighty warriors for God are diminished to walking wounded.

What I have not seen in all my years in the church is the body of Christ reaching out to these hurting people beyond the general "God loves you and forgives your sin." There are some resources for post-abortion healing in a growing number of Para church organizations; for instance it is becoming more common for pregnancy resource centers to provide abortion recovery programs for these wounded individuals. Although I support these programs wholeheartedly, I believe just as strongly that abortion recovery should be a ministry of Christ within His church. As one pastor of a prominent church in our state recently said, "The world can do benevolent deeds, but as Christians we are called to do what only the church can do – reconcile people to Christ." It is recognizing the need for this reconciliation within the church that has driven me to write this book.

My prayer is that in reading this book you will begin, as I did, to see the abortion-affected through God's eyes, with understanding and compassion. I pray that you will share this book with your pastor and other church leaders so they too can begin reconciling these hurting people to Christ.

And finally, if you have been wounded by an abortion, I pray this book will help you to know you are not alone. There are multitudes just like you within the church. If you have believed for years that you are the only Christian that has ever had an abortion, I pray this book banishes that belief forever! I also pray it will be the catalyst for your healing in Christ. He loves you so! The desire of His heart is to reconcile your heart to His. May this book be that first step for you.

In His service,
Mary Comm
President, In Our Midst Ministries, Inc.

1. Study conducted by Dr. Vincent Rue, a clinical psychologist, Dr. David Reardon of the Elliot Institute, and Priscilla Coleman, a researcher at Bowling Green State University. Reported by LifeNews.com 12/1/04.

x

CHAPTER 1

CHRISTIANS DON'T ABORT - OR DO THEY?
UNDERSTANDING WHO CHOOSES ABORTION AND WHY

"No one wants an abortion as she wants an ice-cream cone or a Porsche. She wants an abortion as an animal, caught in a trap, wants to gnaw off its own leg."
                    – Frederica Mathewes-Green[1]

The phone call came on a chilly November afternoon. The amniocentesis showed probable Down Syndrome. Termination of the pregnancy was the doctor's recommendation and a decision had to be made immediately.

Barbara and Russ[2] had planned this pregnancy. They wanted this child and loved him already. But the prognosis of Down Syndrome sent them reeling. Questions flooded their minds: Could they cope with a special needs child? How would they manage the additional medical costs? How would a handicapped baby affect their two year old daughter?

Russ and Barbara researched Down Syndrome. Both of them were pro-life and had been raised attending church. They spoke with a genetics counselor. They sought wise counsel from other Christians and leaders of their church. But every recommendation was the same: termination of the pregnancy (abortion).

On December 5th, Barbara delivered a tiny two pound, ten ounce baby boy through a procedure called "early induction of labor." Their son, fully formed at 26 weeks gestation, was placed in Barbara's arms as the doctor and nurse left the delivery room. Within minutes their baby was dead.

Their lives would never be the same again.

THE BIG PICTURE

Russ and Barbara's story is not rare, but it is one rarely heard. Forget that their abortion was done for medical reasons. The root issues that led them to abort their son were twofold: a lack of understanding of God and the value of every life, and a wrong belief that abortion would solve their problem and end their trial. As people who value the life of the unborn, and and because of the pro-abortion rhetoric we have witnessed over the years, many of us may have a picture in our minds of careless, callous women proudly stomping into a clinic demanding their right to end the life of their unborn children. Nothing could be further from the truth. In fact, the vast majority of people who have abortions

> THE VAST MAJORITY OF PEOPLE WHO HAVE ABORTIONS IN THIS COUNTRY DO SO BECAUSE OF A DANGEROUS COMBINATION OF SOCIETAL PRESSURES, WORLDLY DECEPTIONS, WRONG BELIEFS, AND POOR DECISION-MAKING.

in this country do so because of a dangerous combination of societal pressures, worldly deceptions, wrong beliefs, and poor decision-making. As a result, most of them feel they have no alternative.

THE DYNAMICS OF DECEPTION

Many factors contribute to a woman's decision to choose abortion, not the least of which is living in a me-centered, sex-obsessed, consequence-avoidant society. It is also a society that over the past three decades has saturated the minds of our young people with pro-abortion rhetoric and deception. These people, many of which are merely teens and young adults have heard all their lives that abortion is a woman's right to choose; it's her body and nobody should be able to tell her what to do with it. They've heard the word abortion used so casually without any true explanation of what it is or what the results are - both for the child and for the mother (et al) that they don't even realize - or don't believe - that it ends the life of a child. Abortion has been touted as a "woman's right to choose" by the pro-abortion camp for more than 30 years now, and through every viable medium.

Because abortion has been a part of our culture for so long, and because so many "experts" have debated when life actually begins, life within the womb has been devalued to the point that many men and women (of all ages and backgrounds) will choose this "simple, clinical procedure" known as abortion without even thinking of it as their child. Because the message of society about sex is that "everyone is doing it" – even to the point that abstinence has gotten a bum rap – few young people believe they are even capable of preserving their purity until marriage. Thus even "godly" young couples in church youth groups or preparing for the ministry are sexually active. When the unthinkable happens, they often resort to abortion rather than being caught in their sin, and all the more so when their parents are in the ministry or are well-known in their church. They believe abortion will simply make the problem disappear. They do not realize however that the repercussions are often devastating and life-long.

Though the option of adoption is always readily available, many of those who choose abortion never think about it as a viable option, or if they do, it carries with it too much shame, too much personal sacrifice, or ironically enough, the threat of too much emotional pain. Many people think it would be far too painful to give their baby away... (A hard reality, with lifelong effects of its own.) Why should she put herself through all that when abortion has been sold to her as a casual, easy, simple proce- dure about which no one will ever have to know? Sadly, the young people of our society have been lied to over the past 30+ years by those who would profit from their tragedy, and those of us with the truth have not sufficiently countered those lies with the hard evidence.

3

At this point it would be easy to get into all the moral and political rhetoric here, but the truth of the matter is that the minds of our young men and women have been saturated with the notion over the past three decades that abortion is as safe as a trip to the dentist--much safer than carrying a baby to term--and that it is nothing more than a simple medical procedure that solves a tragic problem.

PERSUASIONS AND PRESSURES

Concerning Singles

The young people of our society don't just have the pro-abortion mainstream media and Planned Parenthood's slick and savvy sex-without-consequences campaign persuading them to abort. The other influences in their lives speak just as loudly, some even louder: like the voice of the boyfriend (unprepared for fatherhood or unwilling to pay child support) who threatens to break up with her if she chooses to have the baby; or the parents that have assured her they would kick her out of the house if she ever came home pregnant; or the girl who is raped by the star quarterback on the football team while on a date or by an anonymous attacker. Continuing with the pregnancy would multiply her shame, and how could she love a baby so brutally conceived? The career-minded woman may have just finished college - a baby would totally disrupt all her plans. The businesswoman has been vying for that big promotion. She believes having a baby now would ruin all her hard work and put an end to all her dreams. There is also the young Christian couple who in a moment of passion makes a bad decision. How can they face their Christian parents or peers at church? How can they bring such shame upon their families? Perhaps her parents are leaders in the church? Perhaps his father is the pastor or her mother is on the women's ministry team....

Concerning Couples

But it doesn't just happen to singles. Married couples abort regularly as well. Perhaps the husband has a violent temper or the couple is struggling in their marriage. The couple that is under financial pressures may consider abortion rather than create more of a hardship for the rest of the family. As it is they are barely making it, and another mouth to feed would put them over the edge. One couple was in seminary and preparing to go out into the ministry. When the wife became pregnant unexpectedly they opted to terminate the pregnancy rather than hinder the ministry to which God had called them. Each of these circumstances is the product of wrong thinking, but even so, the choice to abort is made without any consideration or knowledge of the repercussions to follow.

Concerning Medical Issues

When signs of medical abnormalities appear or the mother has a history of a serious health issue that could potentially threaten her life, abortion is often perceived as the only option. Many doctors will advise their patients to abort rather than to continue with the pregnancy. When the abnormalities seem severe enough even many clergy will support the doctor's position, reinforcing the idea that everyone will be better off if the pregnancy is terminated. With

> "IN AMERICA, MORE THAN 80 PERCENT OF THE BABIES DIAGNOSED PRENATALLY WITH DOWN SYNDROME ARE ABORTED."
>
> --*George F. Will Source: The Augusta Chronicle*

such weighty opinions, often the family and friends will concur, leaving these devastated parents confused, afraid and feeling alone.

Others may simply have an erroneous idea of who God is. For example, one woman I spoke with several years ago believed that God did not want her to suffer through an unwanted pregnancy. Her view of God was completely skewed. She knew in the end God would forgive her for

5

having an abortion, so for her the price was small and acceptable. In her case she would merely confess her sin and all would be forgotten. Sadly, it is never that simple. Yes, God forgives the sin of abortion, but although He forgives, He does not remove the natural consequences.

Whatever the reasons – and there are many – God's people are choosing abortion when faced with an unplanned, ill-timed, or problem pregnancy. For many it is the lesser of two bad situations. They believe abortion will solve their problem and hide their sin or divert their suffering. What they don't realize is

> WHATEVER THE REASONS — AND THERE ARE MANY — GOD'S PEOPLE ARE CHOOSING ABORTION WHEN FACED WITH AN UNPLANNED, ILL-TIMED, OR PROBLEM PREGNANCY.

that while abortion will end the pregnancy, the suffering it brings is greater than any they would have faced had they chosen life. Their problems aren't over but have merely begun. And they are sitting in the pew next to us on Sunday morning, suffering in silence under a shroud of guilt and shame.

STATISTICS AND SCENARIOS

We've discussed who has abortions and why, but we haven't talked about how many. We've established that Christians choose abortions and the reasons they do so, but how many could we possibly be talking about? Can there be that many people within the church that have been wounded by an abortion?

CHART 1:1 STUDIES AND STATISTICS

Recognizing the Number of Post-Abortive in Our Midst

Statistics:[3]

- Half of all pregnancies to American women are unintended; half of these end in abortion.
- In 2002, 1.29 million abortions occurred.
- **At current rates, one in three American women will have at least one abortion by the time she reaches age 45. Half of those will have a second abortion.**
- 88% of abortions occur in the first 12 weeks of pregnancy.
- A broad cross section of U.S. women have abortions.
  - 56% of women having abortions are in their 20s;
  - 61% have one or more children;
  - 67% have never married;
  - 57% are economically disadvantaged;
  - 88% live in a metropolitan area; and
  - **78% report a religious affiliation.**

Studies:[4]

- A recent study showed that 65% of women having abortions experienced multiple post-traumatic stress disorder symptoms and women who are more likely experience a negative reaction
  - (a) Had feelings against abortion prior to the procedure
  - (b) Were pressured to abort
  - (c) Had deeply-felt religious views, or
  - (d) Received little or no counseling prior to the abortion.
    According to this study, the category of women experiencing the greatest percentage of post-abortion trauma issues would be pro-life and/or Christian (religious) women.

Even with such an enormous number of people having been hurt in some way by abortion, most churches have no programs or services specifically designed to meet their needs.

THE MOTHERS

Statistics reveal that at current rates, *one in three women will have at least one abortion by the age of 45, and half of those will have a second abortion.*[5] Statistics also report that approximately 70% of the women choosing abortion align themselves with evangelical Christianity or Roman Catholicism. We also know that some of those that choose abortion come to saving knowledge of Jesus Christ after the fact.

Some of these women made the decision to abort on their own without consulting the father or their parents. However many of them succumbed to the abortion due to extreme pressure or coercion from the father of the baby or from their own parents. Numerous women over the years have told me how their parents took them against their will to have the abortion. They felt powerless against their parents to save their babies.

Sometimes, when the father of the child is involved, he may force, coerce, or manipulate her into having an abortion she does not want. She "gives in" in order to save her relationship with this man, only to despise him afterward. [Evidence suggests that upwards of 80% of relationships fail following abortion.]

THE FATHERS

Many men in our culture have believed the lie that abortion is as safe and easy as a visit to the dentist. They also have a tremendous financial responsibility if the mother were to file for child support. Abortion is the easy way out for everyone involved, or so they think. So either they threaten to leave her if she doesn't abort, or they take her to the clinic either out of a sense of duty to protect her or to make sure the job is done.

Many fathers, however, want their child and they may offer to marry the mother. They hate the fact that their indiscretion resulted in a pregnancy, but they don't want to abort. At this point, the couple may discuss their options, only to come to the realization that they have no other option. If they go through with the pregnancy it may bring immense shame on their families, especially if they are active in the church. The pregnancy may mean the end of their dreams and plans. These fathers become reluctant accomplices to the abortion.

Still other fathers want their child to live, but the mother refuses to carry the child to term. Michael contacted me several years ago when I was living in the state of Texas. He wanted to know how he could prevent his girlfriend from aborting their baby. I had to inform him that at that time he had no legal right to his child until it was born. Michael's girlfriend went through with the abortion. Both his child and his fatherhood were aborted without his consent.

THE GRANDPARENTS, AUNTS AND UNCLES

Sometimes it is the parents of the pregnant couple that either force or recommend the abortion. Their reasons usually fall into one of a few categories: either they want to save their daughter from having to be a teenaged mother or they fear they would have to raise the child themselves. Some make the decision so their daughter's future is not hindered regarding college and a career, and others simply see abortion as the unfortunate solution to a bad situation.

Still others are like Michael in the previous story. They want their grandchild to live but are unable to prevent the abortion.

The same is true of the mother's or father's siblings. If they are involved in the decision-making process or know of the pregnancy and are unable to prevent the abortion, they too will suffer emotionally as a result.

THE FRIENDS

Many times the mother's closest friends are consulted in the decision-making process. The friends that influence her to abort may do so out of ignorance or panic, as I did, or if they have had an abortion themselves, they may encourage her to abort as well. Carol Everett[6], a former abortion clinic owner in Texas, says that every abortion she sold justified her own. It is similar with many friends as well. If they can influence their friend to have an abortion, somehow it makes their own abortion more okay.

THE SIBLINGS

The siblings of that aborted child also suffer the consequences, whether they know of the abortion or not. Their lives are significantly impacted in a number of serious ways, not the least being child abuse, over-protection, neglect, and the list goes on.

Tom and his first wife aborted their third child. The two older children never knew of the abortion, but they were affected nonetheless. Their mother became depressed and violent after the abortion and later got involved in abusive relationships with other men. Eventually when her grandchildren were born she was unable to bond with them. Her children never knew of the abortion, but their lives were deeply affected as a result.

HEALTH PROFESSIONALS

There are also a number of health professionals in our midst that have been involved in the termination of a pregnancy because of fetal abnormalities or due to the health risk to the mother. It doesn't matter how "noble" or seemingly necessary the reason for the abortion, the bottom line is that a child died, and it was their hands that killed. Those in the medical field did not sign on to terminate life; they became doctors and nurses and anesthesiologists in order to save lives, not to end them.

The truth is that good people do horrible things for what at that time appears to be the right reason. Even church leaders often recommend abortion when there is a fetal abnormality or when the woman has been a victim of rape or incest. Their limited knowledge and small faith (or faith in a small God) results in the unthinkable. They've counseled the best they knew how only to realize their error too late.

THE FINAL TALLY

When the tally is tabulated, when all the mothers, fathers, grandparents, aunts, uncles, friends, siblings, and health professionals involved in or affected by an abortion are calculated, the number of abortion-affected people in our midst is overwhelming. Consider on any

> GOOD PEOPLE DO HORRIBLE THINGS FOR WHAT APPEARS TO BE THE RIGHT REASON.

given Sunday morning as you look around at the people of your church, count every third woman. Count every third man. Consider their parents; take into account their children.

In one local bible study group last fall it was discovered that out of ten women five had experienced abortion firsthand. Is there a need for abortion to be addressed within our churches? We have scores of people suffering silently in our midst because of a past abortion. The question is not do we need it, but how can we *not* address it!

1 As quoted in Frederica Mathewes-Green, *Real Choices* (Ben Lomand, CA: Conciliar Press, 1994), 11

2 Some names changed for privacy

3 Alan Guttmacher Institute

4 Study conducted by Dr. Vincent Rue, a clinical psychologist, Dr. David Reardon of the Elliot Institute, and Priscilla Coleman, a researcher at Bowling Green State University. Reported by LifeNews.com 12/1/04.

5 Alan Guttmacher Institute

6 Carol Everett, author of "Blood Money" and Director of The Heidi Group

CHAPTER 2

THE LIES WE HAVE BELIEVED
DEBUNKING THE MYTHS ABOUT ABORTION

"They've made their bed. Now they must lie in it."

– Anonymous Pastor[1]

What Do You Believe About Those that Choose Abortion?

It is easy and all too common for those of us who have never been involved in an abortion to proclaim our disgust for those who have. We can't imagine what would possess a person to end the life of their own child for *any* reason, much less some of those listed previously. We hate abortion and everything it represents. Our righteous anger rises. Our brow furrows. Our tone becomes harsh. We verbalize our disdain for the sin, but often it doesn't stop there. Because we don't understand the sin, we draw our righteous dagger and disembowel the sinner.

Hosea 4:6 says *"My people are destroyed for lack of knowledge."* That's what this book is all about. It is about sharing knowledge of the hidden sin of abortion and its consequences with those that have probably thought little about it beyond a general moral or political viewpoint. What we know and believe about abortion and those that choose it is vital. True

> TRUE KNOWLEDGE LEADS TO UNDERSTANDING. UNDERSTANDING LEADS TO COMPASSION. COMPASSION LEADS TO ACTION — THE VERY ACTION CHRIST WAS MOST KNOWN FOR.

knowledge leads to understanding. Understanding leads to compassion. Compassion leads to action – the very action Christ was most known for – the act of laying down one's life for another caught in sin.

So what do you believe about abortion and those that choose it? Let's look at some of the most common myths pertaining to that question.

COMMON MYTHS ABOUT PEOPLE WHO "CHOOSE" ABORTION

Myth #1. Women who choose to abort do so out of selfishness and arrogance, proudly stomping into the local abortion clinic demanding their legal right to terminate their pregnancy.

The truth more often than not is to the contrary. As quoted earlier, Frederica Mathewes-Green[1] has said, "No one wants an abortion as she wants an ice-cream cone or a Porsche. She wants an abortion as an animal, caught in a trap, wants to gnaw off its own leg." It's a brutal yet fitting description for an excruciating event in the lives of these women. Most of them believe abortion is the lesser of two consequences – if they even have the freedom to make the choice for themselves. Most women have someone else in their life that is pushing them or forcing them to abort. For those for which the choice is theirs, they are making this decision based on their own misinformation coupled with the fear that comes with one of the biggest events in a person's life – pregnancy. If they feel unprepared for parenthood, if they believe their pregnancy will significantly hurt others or their relationship with others, they will choose the seemingly lesser consequence.

The pro-life community has shied away from the term "crisis pregnancy" in recent years because no pregnancy should be viewed as a crisis. Semantics aside, and agreeing that the new life that has been conceived is not itself a crisis, for many people the confirmation they're pregnant does indeed put them in crisis mode. Simply put, they are terrified. Adrenaline begins pumping. Their hands shake. Their voice quivers. Their heart beats faster. Their mind races. Suddenly they can't think clearly. Add to that the fact that time is working against them. They don't have months to make the biggest decision of their lives. Instead they have days or a few weeks at most. For all intents and purposes they are in crisis.

Is it selfishness? For some, yes it certainly is. For others it is self-pres-ervation. For many women it boils down to "It's me or you and I choose me." Is that arrogance? No. But it is infinitely sorrowful.

Myth #2. Only pro-abortion women have abortions.

The sad truth is that many pro-life Christian women have abortions. It's easy to stand on one's principles when one is not faced with the life-altering consequences of pregnancy. It's easy to say, "I would never have an abortion," - until faced with a pregnancy that creates a crisis situation in your life. Until we walk a mile in their shoes we cannot know what they have gone through. We are not called to judge the motives of others or to condemn them for their sin. On the contrary, we are commanded and our responsibility is to love them like Jesus, to be His hands, feet and heart of compassion toward them, reconciling them to Christ, restoring them to a right relationship with God.

The best attitude for those who are non-abortive to embrace is one of gratitude: *There but by the grace of God go I.* This attitude promotes the compassion of Christ and stifles the tendency to be judgmental. It builds bridges instead of walls.

> **IT'S EASY TO SAY, "I WOULD NEVER HAVE AN ABORTION," UNTIL FACED WITH A PREGNANCY THAT CREATES A CRISIS SITUATION IN YOUR LIFE.**

Myth #3. People who choose abortion are taking the easy way out.

The truth is that abortion is never the "easy way out." In fact, the consequences of abortion are often horrific. Abortion affects the whole person – physically, emotionally, and spiritually. The possible side effects that follow abortion are varied and include the following:

Possible Physical Consequences to the Mother:

- Infection

- Infertility

> **THE TRUTH IS THAT ABORTION IS NEVER THE "EASY WAY OUT."**

- Miscarriage in subsequent pregnancies

- Breast cancer

- Injury/Mutilation (e.g. perforated bowel, hysterectomy, etc.)

- Death

Emotional Consequences:

Post-Abortion Syndrome (PAS) is a form of Post Traumatic Stress Syndrome (PTSD). PTSD is the result of having suffered an event so stressful and so traumatic that the person is taken beyond his/her ability to cope in a normal manner. Victims of PTSD are unable to simply resume their lives where they left off before the traumatic event. Instead they experience a variety of reactions that do not go away merely with the passage of time. Although the symptoms of PTSD (and PAS) are varied, and although they may not surface for years after the trauma, they are nonetheless real and should be dealt with.

The events leading up to and including the abortion itself are often of such a traumatic nature that PTSD is often the result. Few if any of those who choose abortion are prepared for its devastating effects.

Possible Symptoms of Post-Abortion Syndrome in Women:

- Depression, Sad Mood, Sudden and Uncontrollable Crying

- Deterioration of Self-Esteem

- Disruption in Interpersonal Relationships (Marital difficulties, divorce, alienating oneself, entering into or remaining in abusive relationships, etc.)

- Intense, Uncontrolled Anger

- Sleep Disturbances (Insomnia, nightmares, etc.)

- Eating Disorders (Anorexia, bulimia, food addiction)

- Sexual Disturbances (Promiscuity, lack of sex drive, pornography addiction, etc.)

- Reduced Motivation (Thinking, "What's the point…?")

- Thoughts of Suicide

- "Anniversary Syndrome" (An increase of symptoms around the time of the anniversary of the abortion and/or the due date of the aborted child.)

- Re-experiencing the Abortion

- Preoccupation with Becoming Pregnant Again (Also called "Replacement Child Syndrome")

- Anxiety over Fertility and Childbearing Issues (Thinking, "God will punish me by not allowing me to have children, or by taking the children I already have.")

- Disruption of the Bonding Process with Present or Future Children

- Survival Guilt (The decision boiled down to a sorrowful conclusion: "It's me or you, and I choose me.")

- Alcohol and Drug Abuse

- Inability to Accept or Offer Forgiveness Pertaining to the Abortion: Bitterness (Often results in a hardness of heart that spills over into many areas of the person's life)

- Other Self-Punishing or Self-Degrading Behaviors: failing to take care of oneself medically or deliberately hurting oneself emotionally and/or physically (This includes cutting/self-mutilation)

- Brief Reactive Psychosis: an episode of drastically distorted reality within two weeks of the abortion

Possible Symptoms of Post-Abortion Syndrome in Men[3]:

• Intense, Uncontrolled Anger

• Depression/Isolation

• Low Self-Esteem; Fragile Ego; Feelings of Inadequacy

• Mistrust of Women (if she got pregnant in order to "trap" him, or if she had the abortion without his consent)

• Difficulty in Establishing and Maintaining Close Relationships with Others; Inability to Commit to Marriage

• Inability To Bond With Subsequent Children, Step-Children, Or Grandchildren

• May Be Overcome With Guilt, Shame, Remorse, Anxiety May Abuse or Become Addicted to Drugs, Alcohol, or Food to Numb the Pain

• May Feel Estranged From God; Unforgivable

• Suicide Ideation

• Sexual Dysfunction Including Impotence and Sexual / Pornography Addiction

• Wounds From His Own Absentee or Abusive Father are Triggered

• Fear of All Kinds: Fear of Failure; Fear of Rejection

• Helplessness

• Higher Rate of Domestic Violence or Child Abuse

Three or more of the symptoms listed above resulting from an abortion, suggest that Post-Abortion Syndrome is present. And because Post-Abortion Syndrome (PAS) is a post-traumatic stress disorder it requires specialized biblical counseling over a period of time with a facilitator trained in this area. The training is not difficult, but it is vital due to the intensity of the feelings associated with these symptoms and because of the tendency toward destructive behaviors and suicide. Also, because of the shame that often accompanies Post-Abortion Syndrome, complete confidentiality and a promise of anonymity is also vital.

Spiritual Consequences:

Sin–any sin–hinders our fellowship with our Heavenly Father.

- *"You rebuke and discipline men for their sin…" Psalm 39:11*
- *"If I had cherished sin in my heart, the Lord would not have listened…" Psalm 66:18*
- *"Many times He delivered them, but they were bent on rebel lion and they wasted away in their sin." Psalm 106:43*

Many people in our churches are wasting away in their sin either because of the intense shame and guilt, or because they are unaware of the connection between the difficulties in their life and their past abortion experience.

If you are a leader in your church one of the most important things you can do is learn to recognize the presenting symptoms of a past unresolved abortion experience. Chances are you're already ministering to some of these people in regard to these subsequent issues resulting from Post-Abortion Syndrome. If two or more of these presenting symptoms are present, gently and compassionately ask if there is an abortion in their past. They may not tell you the truth right away, but the likelihood is better than if you didn't ask the question. Whatever response they give, shower them with the love and grace of Christ and remind them that our God is a God of forgiveness and reconciliation.

CHART 2:1 PRESENTING SYMPTOMS OF A PAST UNRESOLVED ABORTION EXPERIENCE

- Depression
- Uncontrolled Anger
- Marital problems
- Relationship problems
- Self-Esteem issues
- Sexual problems (lack of interest in sex, fear of intimacy, pro-miscuity, or pornography addiction)
- Drug and/or alcohol abuse
- Cutting (Self-mutilation)
- Eating Disorders (anorexia, bulimia, food addictions)
- Self-destructive thoughts or behaviors
- Thoughts of suicide

The probability is that you are already counseling people in your church that are post-abortive. Many people will consult their pastor for counseling for these issues (listed above) without even realizing their abortion is the root cause for the pain in their lives. Others may be in denial about their abortions, having convinced themselves it was the right choice to make given the circumstances. Those that do acknowledge that their abortion was wrong are silenced by shame and the fear of being judged or condemned.

Myth #4. The way to stop abortion is to make it illegal again.

The most effective deterrent to abortion is the changing of hearts which is accomplished only through Jesus Christ and perpetuated by the changed lives of those He has healed from Post-Abortion Syndrome. The illegalization of abortion would certainly decrease the number of abortions, but the battle would inevitably heat up between the pro-life and pro-abortion camps. Likewise illegal abortions would continue to take place increasing the risk of mutilations and deaths of the women seeking them. No, the answer is not simply to change the laws of our land; the answer is to facilitate healing in the lives of those wounded by abortion and give them an opportunity to declare how abortion hurt them and how Jesus healed them. When people begin to see abortion for what it really is and that it doesn't help women but hurts them and everyone around them, then and only then will the perspectives of abortion begin to change in this country. And the best part is that God will receive the glory for it!

COMMON MYTHS ABOUT ABORTION IN GENERAL:

Myth #1. Having an abortion is as safe as going to the dentist.
There is nothing safe about abortion! [See list of physical and emotional symptoms discussed earlier.]

Myth #2. Abortion solves the problem of an unplanned or unwanted pregnancy.
Considering the possible and often probable consequences listed above, the natural and logical conclusion would then be that instead of solving the problem, abortion merely heaps pain upon pain, making a difficult situation infinitely worse.

Myth #3. Abortion solves the problem of rape.
Let's settle this once and for all. *There is never a reason to terminate the life of an unborn child through abortion.* The predominant reason

for this strong conviction is that God is the Creator and Sustainer of all life. Life and death are and should be in His hands. The decision to allow a life to continue or not should rest solely in the mind and will of God. Period. For mankind to take these matters into his own hand is to confess one of two things: (1) that there is no God, or (2) that God is not big enough or wise enough or kind enough to manage His Creation. If you, as a Christian, believe there is ever a situation that warrants an abortion you are basically saying, "This one must have slipped by God; it's up to us to clean up His mess." This belief reveals how big your God is to you. I for one will attest to the fact that my God is huge! Nothing escapes His notice. Nothing slips past Him in the night. What He allows He does so for a reason and a purpose, and no life – no matter how young, how old, how imperfect or inopportune – is a mistake. And it is certainly not a mistake we need to mend.

I've said it before but it bears repeating: the natural and logical conclusion would then be that instead of solving the problem, abortion merely heaps pain upon pain, making a difficult situation infinitely worse. Abortion re-victimizes the victim.

On the contrary, the alternative (having the baby) becomes a testimony to the love and grace of Jesus Christ and His ability to redeem even the most unimaginable set of circumstances.

Myth #4. Abortion solves the problem of incest.
Again, as in the case of rape, abortion re-victimizes the victim. In addition, abortion allows the perpetrator of the incest to continue assaulting the child without fear of being found out.

Myth #5. Abortion only affects the mother of the baby.
We have already discussed the others who are affected:
• The father of the baby
• The parents of the mother and father

- The siblings of the aborted child (whether they ever learn of the abortion or not)
- Future grandchildren *(Note: Abortion reaches into the next generation.)*
- The friends of the mother and father
- The abortion clinic personnel, including the office and medical staff

The truth is that abortion affects every life it touches.

Myth #6. The unwanted baby is better off dead.

This line of thinking is a coping mechanism that enables the woman to live with her decision to end the life of her unborn child. The fact is that because it is God who creates life, it is also God who should determine the time of each person's physical death.

Further, because of the high incidence of infertility, there are always couples waiting to adopt newborns. So in effect, the truth is that no child is unwanted.

Myth #7. Abortion decreases the incidences of child abuse.

In 1998 Dr. Theresa Burke, a psychotherapist, and Dr. David Reardon, a biomedical ethicist and the director of the Elliot Institute, reported a significant increase in child abuse in their article titled, *Abortion Trauma and Child Abuse*, showing that the occurrence of child abuse has actually risen significantly since abortion became legal in 1970:

> "Experts agree that during the past 25 years the rate of child abuse has increased dramatically. Between 1976 and 1987 alone, there was a 330% increase in reported cases of child abuse. While a portion of this increase is due to better report-ing, experts agree that these figures reflect a real trend toward ever higher rates of abuse."[2]

Because of the mental and emotional pain suffered by the post-abortive woman or man, even while in the throes of denial, there is an increased tendency toward neglecting and abusing existing or subsequent children.

KNOWLEDGE IS POWER

Jesus said, *"The truth will set you free."* (John 8:32) That statement is never more true than in the light of what the church has believed about abortion. When we finally begin to see abortion, the abortion decision, and those that are wounded by abortion in the light of truth, the freedom will ripple through our congregations like a tidal wave, transforming our church families and our nation to the glory of Jesus Christ. May we be free indeed!

Questions to Ask Yourself About Your Abortion Belief System:
• What do I believe about abortion?
• What feelings does abortion stir in me?
• How much do I know and what has my source of information been?
• What language do I use when discussing abortion?

Realize, before you can minister to those wounded by abortion, *you must know where you stand.* Before you can minister to those wounded by abortion, you must have an accurate understanding of the issue.... *Understanding that leads to compassion.*

CHART 2:2 ABORTION MYTHS: UNCOVERING THE LIES WE HAVE BELIEVED

Myth/Misperception/Wrong Belief	The Truth
Women who choose abortion do so out of selfishness and arrogance.	Many women choose abortion due to fear, wrong beliefs about abortion, or because of the pressures from outside influences.
Only pro-choice people have abortions.	The reality of an ill-timed pregnancy can often outweigh a person's pro-life beliefs when it becomes a personal experience.
Abortion is the "easy way out."	There is nothing "easy" about making the decision to abort or about the abortion procedure. This process is both frightening and painful, and it brings with it life-altering consequences. (See list of PAS symptoms)
Having an abortion is as safe as going to the dentist.	Abortion ends the life of many women each year. Others are left mutilated or otherwise injured or damaged. (See list of possible physical side-effects)
It's not a baby; it's merely a blob of tissue.	Life begins at conception! God is the Creator of life and He "knew" us from the womb. Psalm 139
Its a woman's body and no one should be able to tell her what to do with it. ("Woman's Right to Choose")	There are two bodies involved in abortion: the mother's and the baby's. The baby's life is just as valuable as the mother's because both were created by God.
The abortion issue is all about saving the baby.	Abortion affects every life it touches. As such, this is an issue that is not only about

Myth/Misperception/Wrong Belief	The Truth
	the baby, but about the mother, father, grandparents, siblings, other family, and friends as well as the medical personnel. For those abortions that have already occurred, the baby is in heaven with Jesus; it is those left behind that must live with the consequences.
Abortion solves the problem of an unplanned or ill-timed pregnancy.	Abortion doesn't solve anything. It may end the pregnancy, but with it comes a whole new set of problems and crises.
Abortion solves the problem of rape and incest.	For both victims the abortion re-victimizes her. Additionally, abortion allows the perpetrator of incest to continue violating his young victim in secret.
The way to stop abortion is to make it illegal again.	Although making abortion illegal again would decrease the number of abortions each year, it is only through the changing of hearts and perspectives that abortion will become rare.
Abortion is okay in certain circumstances (e.g. genetic defect, health-risk to mother, etc.)	Abortion is never okay! To recommend abortion is to suggest that God has made a mistake and that He needs our help in cleaning things up! God doesn't make mistakes and all events serve His will! God can redeem any situation when it is surrendered to Him. (See Romans 8:28, 29)

CHART 2:3 WHY WOMEN CHOOSE ABORTION

Reasoning	Self	Boyfriend	Parents	Husband	Friend	Doctor	Clergy
Interruption of Plans: College, Career, High School,Ministry (38%)[4]	X	X	X	X	X		
Unprepared to Parent (30%) /Single Parent (48%)	X	X	X				
Finances (73%)	X	X	X	X			
Previous Threats in the Event of Teen Pregnancy			X				
Perceived Medical Threat to Mother's Life (12%)	X	X	X	X	X	X	X
Perceived Genetic Defect or Concern for Health of Fetus (13%)	X	X	X	X	X	X	X
Relationship Problems (48%)	X		X	X			
Domestic Abuse	X		X		X		
Shame/Guilt/Fear	X	X	X		X	X	
Validation of Previous Abortion		X	X	X	X		
Have All the Children They Want (40%)	X	X	X	X	X		
Infidelity	X	X			X		
Rape/Incest (1%)	X		X	X	X	X	X

1: Frederica Mathewes-Green: As quoted in Frederica Mathewes-Green, Real Choices (Ben Lomand, CA: Conciliar Press, 1994), 11

2: Abortion Trauma and Child Abuse: Abortion Trauma and Child Abuse, Theresa Burke, Ph.D and David Reardon, Ph.D. http://www.abortionfacts.com/reardon/abortion_and_child_abuse.asp

3: PAS Symptoms in Men: Gregory Hasek, MA/MFT LPC, Executive Director, Misty Mountain Family Counseling Center

4: Percentages on Chart 2:3: Reasons U.S. Women Have Abortions: Quantitative and Qualitative Perspectives; Guttmacher Institute, New York.

CHAPTER 3

ABORTION'S HOLD ON THOSE IT TOUCHES
COMMON REACTIONS AND RESPONSES TO ABORTION

Common (handwritten margin note)

> *"I left the clinic knowing I would never be the same again. I spiralled into a deep depression and turned to alcohol, drugs, food and self-harming to numb me from the pain. I isolated myself from my friends. I lived in a world of my own – my own secret world of shame. I couldn't cope with what I had done. I couldn't live in my brokenness. The only solution in my mind was to end my life."*
>
> *– Shelly*

In the introduction to this book we discussed how many people have been involved in and affected by abortion. Statistics, you'll remember, report one in three women will have at least one abortion by the age of 45. Add to that number the babies' fathers, grandparents, aunts, uncles, siblings, friends of the family, medical personnel, etc., and the number rises staggeringly. So if that many people within the church have been affected by abortion, why don't we know about it? Why haven't they come forward? If so many people have been hurt by abortion, shouldn't it be obvious?

You would think so. But the reality is that many of those wounded by abortion don't even realize their abortion is the cause of their pain. They've been deceived and because of their own self-protective denial they haven't made the connection between their abortion and their pain. Add to that the fact that many non-abortive people have little or no understanding of the abortion issue. Many non-abortive Christians innocently make the mistake of making comments like, "I just don't

29

see how anyone could do such a thing...." What this communicates to those who've had abortions is that this is not a safe place in which to share their pain. Because abortion is a shame-based sin, the post-abortive person that has emerged from denial already feels self-condemnation. The natural fear and conclusion then is that those around them within the church are also going to judge and condemn them. And in many instances they would be right in that assumption.

To better understand what I'm talking about, let's examine the three initial responses of the post-abortive person.

INITIAL REACTIONS/LASTING EFFECTS OF ABORTION

My family and I live in the great state of Oklahoma, smack in the center of tornado alley. On May 3, 1999 we had one of those rare multi-state tornado events that people still talk about today, years later. The most powerful tornado in recorded history began forming to the southwest of our fair city and we watched the constant television coverage in awe and wonder as the twister intensified in both size and strength. Within just a few hours and with wind speeds topping out at 318 miles per hour, the tornado decimated over 2,600 homes and businesses and damaged another eight thousand buildings. At least thirty-six people lost their lives in Oklahoma that night and countless others sustained injuries.

My sister and her family were directly in the path of this killer tornado, measuring an F5 on the Fujita scale. Three days after the storm I was allowed past the National Guard barricades and was relieved to find my sister's home mostly in tact. There were holes in the roof and the windows were blown out. A two-by-four plank remained implanted in the exterior wall of her garage and the interior of her home was littered with a variety of debris. But considering the homes directly behind her house had been reduced to unrecognizable piles of rubble,

I was relieved. The storm had been horrible, but her house was still standing. She and her husband would be able to pick up the pieces and go on with their lives.

I relate this story because there are some striking correlations between this tornado event and the event of abortion in many people's lives. While I experienced great relief upon seeing my sister's home, what we learned a short time later, after the house had been inspected for structural damage, was that many of the supporting rods in the exterior walls of her house had been broken during the sudden change in air pressure as the storm passed by. As a result every brick had to be removed from her house, the rods replaced, and new bricks laid. In all, the damage to her house totaled over $50,000 and the repairs took over six months to complete. Had the walls not been inspected, over time they would have begun to crumble under the weight of the roof, the natural pull of gravity, and in the wake of later storms.

For many people that experience an abortion, their initial response is relief. The "storm" – the crisis – has passed. It was horrible, but it's over now. They believe they can simply pick up the pieces and go on with their lives. The trouble is, there are no inspectors to assess the structural damage this storm has caused in their heart, soul, and spirit. Unlike my sister's house, these people are left with undetected internal damage that left untended, results in a crumbling affect. They enter into a state of denial, unaware of the reasons for many of the painful (Post-Abortion Syndrome) issues that begin to wreak havoc in their lives.

Still others respond to abortion like the owners of the homes in my sister's neighborhood that were reduced to rubble. These people, like Shelly, know immediately that their lives have been completely decimated and that they will never be the same again. There is no denial for them. They know full well what has occurred, and as much as they wish they could go back and undo it, the deed has been done and they

have the rest of their lives to live with the regret, remorse, and repercussions of their decision.

Although the actual reactions and consequences of abortion are as
individual as the people who experience abortion, there are some basic
norms that are considered quite common.

INITIAL REACTIONS

Relief Leading to Denial

There are three basic initial reactions to abortion. The first is relief
leading to denial. The crisis has passed. It was horrible, but s/he survived it and now s/he can go on with his/her life. This is the onset of
denial, a self-protective state which allows the individual to carry on
with life as though nothing has happened. Denial can last anywhere
from a few hours to 40 years or more. Until the denial is broken and
the abortion is faced, healing cannot take place. Even within the con-
straints of denial however, symptoms of Post-Abortion Syndrome may
surface. Some of the most common reactions at this point are self-
destructive behaviors such as abusing drugs, alcohol, or food; entering
into destructive relationships; neglecting health issues; experiencing
unexplained depression or rage; or behaving in ways that bring about
unrelated consequences (such as poor job performance resulting in
being fired, etc.).

Relief Followed by Grief

The second initial reaction to abortion is relief followed by a realization
of what s/he has done. Upon facing this realization, s/he either goes into
denial in order to protect his/herself from the overwhelming emotions, or
s/he enters into deep emotional distress.

Immediate Regret and Utter Devastation

The third initial reaction is immediate regret and utter devastation. This woman or man probably went into the abortion procedure knowing it was wrong, but for whatever reason felt powerless to make any other choice. Often s/he will regret the decision before the procedure is even complete. The woman may even try to stop the procedure after it has begun, only to be restrained and/or comforted by a reminder that it will all be over soon. Unfortunately, these words will hold no comfort for her as she knows now how desperately she wants her baby back - but it's too late. When the realization sinks in that there is no turning back this mother or father knows her/his life will never be the same again. The grief is unbearable. The guilt is overwhelming. And shame sets in to secure that the secret is kept locked away. For this man and woman, Post-Abortion Syndrome sets in immediately and his/her world is turned upside down.

Because of the stronghold of shame, guilt, and condemnation that accompanies abortion, these people are held captive by their sin. Often they have told very few people if anyone of their past. They struggle to carry the burden of their sin alone, yet because of the severity of Post-Abortion Syndrome, most are unable to experience any degree of freedom from it.

In late 2004 I started a ministry, appropriately called *In Our Midst Ministries, Inc.*, for the dual purposes of raising awareness in the church regarding those suffering silently due to a past abortion, and equipping churches with the knowledge and information needed to meet these hurting people at the point of their need. The staff of In Our Midst Ministries is available to anyone interested in being Christ to the abortion-affected. I invite you to visit our web site or contact our home office for more information (see contact information in the back of this book). We are here to serve you as you seek to minister Christ's love, forgiveness and reconciliation to them.

CHART 3:1 A COMPARISON

PAS Symptoms in Women	PAS Symptoms in Men[1]
Uncharacteristic and uncontrolled anger or bitterness	Uncontrolled anger (as an "acceptable" method of processing grief)
Sleep disturbances (insomnia, nightmares, etc.)	A higher rate of domestic violence and child abuse may occur as a result of that anger
Depression, sad mood, or sudden and uncontrollable crying	Depression
Thoughts of suicide	Suicide Ideation
Onset of anxiety or other personality disorders Anxiety over fertility and childbearing issues	Anxiety
Disruption in interpersonal relationships (e.g. marital problems, divorce, inability to bond with subsequent children and grandchildren, inability to let people get "close," etc.)	Inability to bond or commit to current or future partner Inability to bond with subsequent children, grandchildren, or step-children Isolation
Feelings of unworthiness in their relationship with God	Inability to bond with God (The Father)
Inability to accept or offer forgiveness pertaining to the abortion	Fragile ego resulting in refusal to admit wrongs
Reduced motivation	Feelings of inadequacy, especially as a leader
Overwhelming feelings of shame, guilt, and self-condemnation	Overwhelming feelings of shame and guilt as a result of not protecting or providing for their child.

PAS Symptoms in Women	PAS Symptoms in Men
Sexual Dysfunction (avoidance of sex, promiscuity, sexual addiction, etc.)	Sexual dysfunction including impotence
Addictions to drugs (prescription or illegal drugs), alcohol, food, or other self-medicating practices	Addictions of all kinds especially sex addiction
Eating Disorders (bulimia, anorexia, food addictions)	Father wounds can be triggered as a result of lost fatherhood.
Deterioration of self-esteem	Low self-esteem
Fear of condemnation or of being rejected or judged by others (especially in the church)	Fear of all kinds, such as fear of rejection and failure
Self-punishing or self-degrading behaviors (e.g. cutting; failure to pursue medical attention, etc.)	Helplessness
Preoccupation with becoming pregnant again	Mistrust of women as a result of being kept out of the choice to abort or if she got pregnant in order to trap him
Anniversary Syndrome	
Re-experiencing the abortion	
Brief reactive psychosis	

1: Greg Hasek, Misty Mountain Family Counseling

CHAPTER 4

SUFFERING SILENTLY IN OUR MIDST
WHY POST-ABORTIVE CHRISTIANS DON'T SEEK HEALING FROM THEIR ABORTIONS

> *"The first night after the abortion I knew I would never be the same.... I couldn't tell anyone.... The secret pain, guilt, and shame were too much to live with everyday."*
>
> *– Greg*

Greg was a Christian when he drove his pregnant girlfriend to have an abortion. His relief was short-lived however, and within the first twenty-four hours following the procedure he knew his life was forever changed. But where does a Christian go for help when s/he has just ended the life of her/his unborn child? If he had been a member of your church would he have been able to share his sorrow and regret openly? What kind of comfort and guidance would he have received?

Because having had or having been involved in an abortion is a shame-based sin, the accompanying emotions are incredibly strong. Those that live with this shame fear being judged harshly, condemned critically, or rejected completely. Thus it takes an enormous amount of courage for a post-abortive person to tell someone of their secret sin, and all the more when that other person is a Christian.

Even with all the recovery programs established within many evangelical churches in recent years, most churches still operate under the guise that "we are fine because we're Christians." Instead of functioning like a hospital emergency room (which would be more

> **INSTEAD OF FUNCTIONING LIKE A HOSPITAL EMERGENCY ROOM, MANY CHURCHES CONTINUE TO FUNCTION MORE LIKE A COUNTRY CLUB.**

appropriate in many cases), many churches continue to function more like a country club. People are ashamed of the condition of their lives, so they put on a happy face and pretend everything is okay for their brief time at church. It's no wonder then why few Christians share their abortion experiences with other Christians.

IS IT ANY WONDER?

Sadly, most Christians in this situation will seek help outside the church long before they will share this kind of secret with their Christian peers – if they seek help at all. Why? Don't they know we will love them in spite of their sin? Don't they know we will embrace them and show them the grace and kindness of Christ? No. The hard truth is that when abortion is the sin issue, they don't want *anyone* to know what they've done, and least of all their Christian peers. And honestly, the church does not have the best reputation for embracing sinners when the offense is of this nature. Sexual sin has always been the most devastating issue for the church to deal with, and understandably so.

In the days of Christ, the religious leaders were quick to stone those caught in sexual sin. Take the woman caught in adultery in John 8 for example. They brought her to Jesus with stones in hand. In more recent centuries churches have excommunicated those in their midst that committed such heinous crimes, shaming them publicly for their indiscretion and casting them out ceremonially. And more recently still, churches have split over such matters. No, sadly the church doesn't have the best track record in dealing with such weighty issues.

What that means, however, is that we have lots of room for improvement! As we begin to see and understand the truth of abortion we can begin to change our responses to it in our communities and in our churches.

TWO SIDES OF THE SAME COIN

When the sin is abortion, there are actually two positions to consider when examining the whys and wherefores of the reconciliation process – those that have committed the sin of abortion and those that have the responsibility for loving them like Jesus.

THE ONE CAUGHT IN SIN

Let's look first into the thought processes of the one involved in an abortion. As mentioned previously, abortion is a shame-based sin. No one – especially a Christian – wants to admit they've been a party to an abortion, whether they are the mother that submitted to it or the father or grandparents that coerced it or the friend that encouraged it. Beyond their not wanting anyone to know, they may still be in denial about the abortion – not that they've had one, but denial that it was the wrong choice. For many people, some Christians included, they have so convinced themselves that what they did was the right thing for the right reason, that they have made peace with the abortion. Because they are in denial, they do not feel there is anything to deal with. Many of them have even made peace with God over the abortion within their denial and feel that He has forgiven them. Neither God's forgiveness in this context nor their denial, however, diminish this sin's hold on their lives. The consequences of their action are usually very evident in their life, but because of their denial they do not attribute those consequences to the abortion. As a result they do not see the need to seek help for the abortion.

Other Christians may have come out of denial and admitted their abortion was the wrong thing; they have confessed it to God, asking for His forgiveness. In doing so, many people feel that's all they need to do. They believe that since God has forgiven them the rest is best

39

left in the past. They are deeply afraid of facing that abortion experience again. What they do not realize however, is that receiving God's
forgiveness is simply not enough in most cases to heal their life of
the devastation this abortion
has brought upon them. I do
not say this to in any way
minimize God's forgiveness.
I simply mean that there are
many layers of woundedness,

> RECEIVING GOD'S FORGIVENESS IS
> SIMPLY NOT ENOUGH...THERE ARE
> MANY LAYERS OF WOUNDEDNESS,
> MANY AREAS NEEDING FORGIVE-
> NESS, HEALING AND RESTORATION.

many areas needing forgiveness, healing, and restoration that need
to be addressed before complete healing can be attained. Accepting
God's forgiveness is a huge step in this process, but because of the
overwhelming effects associated with this post-traumatic stress disorder, in most instances the post-abortive person needs to go through a
process dealing with these various areas of woundedness.

Still others believe their sin is beyond God's ability to forgive or that
they don't deserve to be forgiven. When the pastor of your church says
something from the pulpit such as, "No matter what you've done, God
will forgive you...," the abortion-affected are thinking to themselves,
but you don't know what I've done. Their condemnation and guilt is so
great they believe there is not enough grace to cover this sin.

The fourth factor in their unwillingness or inability to seek help from
those in the church is that the church is often not considered a "safe"
place in which to share this pain. If the only time your church addresses
abortion is in regard to Sanctity of Human Life Sunday or in regard
to the lost lives of the unborn, the post-abortive people in your midst
will most likely not feel safe in sharing their abortion experience. (We
will address the issue of safety in the church in a later chapter.) In fact,
if your church is silent on the issue of abortion (from a personal stand-
point), that silence speaks volumes to the post-abortive in your midst.

It reinforces their belief that this sin is too big and this church is an unsafe place in which to share their pain.

Likewise, if those in your church speak about abortion (on a social level) from the viewpoint of, "I just can't understand how anyone could end the life of their own baby," that is another major indicator to the post-abortive person that it is not safe to share their pain. Their fear is that they will be judged harshly or condemned, when what they need is understanding and compassion. If the people in your church hold to that idea, the abortion-wounded will not share this secret that has so devastated their life.

✦ THE ONE CALLED TO RESTORE

Galatians 6:1 admonishes us "who are spiritual" to restore such a one caught in any trespass *"in a spirit of gentleness."* In the next verse the apostle Paul goes on to tell us to *"Bear one another's burdens"* thereby fulfilling the law of Christ. How can we restore them if they won't share the secret of their abortion with us? How can we bear their burdens if they won't tell us what their burdens are?

Since they are "the weaker brother" in this case the responsibility lies with us to do all we can to minister to their needs. In the case of ministering to the abortion-affected that means we must do whatever we can to prove ourselves trustworthy. We must do whatever is within our ability – by the empowerment of the Holy Spirit – to create a safe environment within our churches. (I will discuss how to accomplish this in more detail in a later chapter.) By proving ourselves compassionate stewards of God's grace in regard to the abortion issue as it pertains to those wounded by it in our midst, we are being

> *"BROTHERS, IF ANYONE IS CAUGHT IN ANY TRANSGRESSION, YOU WHO ARE SPIRITUAL SHOULD RESTORE HIM IN A SPIRIT OF GENTLENESS. KEEP WATCH ON YOURSELF, LEST YOU TOO BE TEMPTED." GALATIANS 6:1*

41

Christ to them. As they begin to trust us to deal gently with them in this sin they will begin to walk in His freedom from the bondage of condemnation,

> WE MUST DO WHATEVER WE CAN TO PROVE OURSELVES TRUSTWORTHY... TO CREATE A SAFE ENVIRONMENT WITHIN OUR CHURCHES.

guilt, and shame. As Jesus heals their broken heart, soul, and spirit they will be free to be what He created them to be: bold ministers of His grace and mercy to the glory of God the Father and Christ the Son.

But before we get too carried away, we have our work cut out for us!

CHAPTER 5

OUR RECORD/OUR WRONGS – AND HOW TO CORRECT THEM
HOW THE CHURCH HAS MISSED THE MARK AND WHAT WE CAN DO TO AFFECT CHANGE

> *"I feel so judged by anyone that condemns those who would make the choice to abort."*
>
> *– Anonymous*

PREPARING THE WAY

Any surgeon will tell you that before every surgery there is a flurry of activity. The operating room is prepared – cleaned from floor to ceiling. The appropriate tools are sterilized and laid out. The team of medical professionals cleanses their hands and dons sterile clothing, face masks, and gloves. The room is well lit, with the most concentrated light shining on the operating table where the patient will lie. Hopefully, the surgeon and medical team will be rested and ready to give their best for the sake of the patient.

Making our churches ready to minister to the abortion-affected is no less complex. We must begin by cleaning house. We begin to do that first by assessing what we've done in the past regarding the issue of abortion. What has worked? What has failed? What can we do to affect a positive change and create a safe environment for the post-abortive to share their pain with us?

43

OUR RESPONSE TO ABORTION SO FAR

In our home there is my husband, myself, our two children, and the center of the universe – our Yorkshire Terrier affectionately named Socrates. If you know anything about Yorkies, you know they are strong-willed enough to make Dr. James Dobson cry, and ours is no exception. Amazingly he knows right from wrong in many instances, and whenever the mood strikes him he blatantly chooses to do wrong. When he is caught – and he is always caught – he hears "What did you do?" from whoever catches him. This phrase is said in a certain deep, strong tone of voice that each of us has mastered. His response is always the same. He hangs his head, tucks his little snippet of a tail, his whole body seeming burdened by guilt. For the record that's not what I'm going for here.

We need to be able to look back over our past actions and assess them from our current understanding of truth without berating ourselves or defending them at all costs. No one always gets everything right, and the church is certainly no exception to this rule. Likewise, what we began doing three decades ago was all we knew to do based on the limited amount of information we possessed at the time. Now, with over thirty years of legalized abortion under our belt we have a lot more information. And yes, we are well overdue for some self-examination regarding our responses to the abortion issue and to those that have been affected by abortion.

> WE NEED TO BE ABLE TO LOOK BACK OVER OUR PAST ACTIONS AND ASSESS THEM FROM OUR CURRENT UNDERSTANDING OF TRUTH WITHOUT BERATING OURSELVES OR DEFENDING THEM AT ALL COSTS.

IN THE BEGINNING...

Since the beginning of legalized abortion and continuing for these three decades we have focused almost solely on saving the babies. Quite frankly, that tactic hasn't had the desired affect. It has produced some positive results, but in the end by placing our focus there we have pitted the mother against her baby, and because we are siding with the baby, we have pitted her against us (and Christ) as well. The time for turning the focus to the mother and father of the baby is long overdue. We need to begin to come alongside the parents in their unplanned pregnancy, loving and accepting them in spite of their sin as Christ modeled. Taking that new perspective into consideration, let's take a look at some of the ways we have attempted to help make abortion rare.

LET'S START WITH A SIGN

Years ago the pro-life movement set about to do whatever could be done to prevent more people from choosing abortion. As a result, pro-lifers from practically every walk of life, regardless of religious affiliation, took up their signs and picketed and protested abortion clinics. When the abortion clinics took them to task on this legally, the protestors toned-down their rallies and began gathering to pray. As women arrived at the clinics for their abortions, the protestors – or pray-ers would offer any word they could to try to dissuade these women from taking the lives of their unborn children. On occasion a woman would indeed change her mind and both she and her baby were snatched from the jaws of abortion.

While those sidewalk converts have been great victories, I would like to share a different perspective, a far greater reaching impact of those protests and prayer vigils.

Back in the 80's, when I lived in the Dallas area, occasionally these protests would be picked up by the local media. On one such evening the reporter spoke vile words detailing the behavior of the hate-mongering, law-breaking protestors. The actions of these criminal offenders were, in the reporter's estimation, violating the rights of others to exercise the reproductive freedoms granted these women by the highest court in our land.

Strangely enough, the video footage of the arrest of these lawbreaking vigilantes looked nothing like what the reporter was reporting. What I heard with my ears didn't correspond at all with what I saw with my eyes. The pictures flashing across my television screen were of docile, compliant men and women, handcuffed behind their backs, being dragged brutally across the floor without struggling in the least. Their expressions were pained, but not belligerent. While the news reporter told one story, the pictures told another.

My point is this: as we have exercised our right of free speech and religion, even with the purest of motivations, the greater impact has been a detrimental one in most cases. Yes, a few lives have been saved as a result of those protestors' efforts and I would never diminish the importance of that. However, we must consider how many more people have rejected Christians and Christianity because of those protests and how the media portrayed us. Was the world shown how kind, loving, and compassionate Christians are, or did we merely give a sometimes biased liberal media ammunition with which to portray us as hate-mongering extremists? Have our protests furthered the cause of Christ or have they driven those we were hoping to help further away?

For the most part even at the clinic locations our protesting didn't draw these wounded people to Christ. The women that walked past a group of Christians praying and pleading will hear the words spoken to them that day for the rest of their lives. Will those words draw them to Jesus and to those of us that bear His name, or will those words echo guilt and shame? Did we build bridges inviting them to bring their burden to us or did we create chasms that they believe were lined with judgmental assessments and condemnation?

There are still organized pro-life groups that picket, protest and hold prayer vigils at clinics. Do I agree with their tactics? No. Do I believe they are doing "some" good on some level? Possibly. Do I believe their efforts are doing more harm than good? For the most part, yes. The only exception I would make to this is when the signs held up are along the lines of a personal testimony. One woman affiliated with the Silent No More Campaign recently told me of her own methods of demonstrating at clinics. She holds a sign that says, "I REGRET MY ABORTION." I cannot criticize this tactic. It is coming from a humble heart pertaining to her personal abortion experience. Likewise I seriously doubt the media would cover such an event!

While I deeply respect and acknowledge the value of such demonstrations, I would still caution those that would participate in them. Standing in front of a clinic as women walk in for an abortion is an extremely emotional setting. If you have been wounded by an abortion, keeping control of your emotions will be incredibly difficult. (This is putting it mildly.) My bottom line advice on this situation would be this: If you feel that God has called you to demonstrate by sharing that you regret your abortion, and if you can do so with His empowering, keeping your emotions in check, then go for it. Likewise, realize the spiritual struggle will be intense and one way or another, the impact of it will be enormous. Make sure it is an impact for Christ.

PICTURE THIS!

It's a beautiful spring day. You and a co-worker have decided to walk to the park for lunch. The sounds of happy children playing on the swing set behind you hang happily in the air. You've just taken the first bite of your sandwich when a truck stops at the light in front of you. Plastered on the side of the truck is a billboard size photo of an aborted fetus, head disembodied, limbs mangled and bloody.

Let's say your friend was pro-choice. Do you think seeing that dismembered baby would change his/her mind? Many people that choose abortion also choose to believe – for the sake of self-preservation – that the fetus is merely a blob of tissue as they've been told. For some, seeing the truth of what they aborted can indeed set the record straight. It can also send them to an inpatient program at the local psychiatric ward, or worse, it can be the thing that provokes them to commit suicide. They may already regret their abortion, but have not found healing in Christ. What is our responsibility where they are concerned – especially if we are not providing abortion recovery at our church?

What about the innocent children that see those pictures? Will the pictures of aborted babies be their introduction to "the birds and the bees?"

My question then is: What do the abortion trucks and billboards accomplish? Again, do they draw people to Christ? Do they tell people the truth on a level that is constructive? No, graphic photos whether on trucks or billboards or web sites do not draw the wounded to Christ. We must share the facts and our beliefs about abortion but we must do so responsibly.

SANCTITY OF HUMAN LIFE SUNDAY

Ah, now we're getting somewhere! Does your pastor commemorate Sanctity of Human Life Sunday each January? If so, pat him on the back and encourage him! It takes a lot of courage to bring up the issue of unplanned pregnancy that one Sunday when it's pretty much a taboo subject the rest of the year. However, just the fact that it is a taboo subject at all is a red flag.

Help your pastor to see that talking only about the preciousness of life or the wrongness of abortion heaps condemnation on those for whom the choice has already been made. If they are left out of the presentation, if there is not a plea to the abortion-affected and how they can find forgiveness, healing, and restoration in Christ, then the logical conclusion they will draw is that this church is not a safe place in which to share their secret and/or that their sin is indeed unforgivable.

If that is the case, give your pastor a copy of this book and encourage him to talk about unplanned pregnancies and sexual sins more often. Help him to become educated on the entire "life" issue, including abortion and its affects on the living survivors. Help him to understand who has abortions, why they choose them, and how many of the people in his congregation are most likely suffering silently because of abortion. Encourage him to begin creating a safe environment in your church – one in which the people have a compassionate understanding toward those wounded by abortion; a church that has a reputation for loving and restoring sinners no matter how detestable their sin.

If he has the courage to mention Sanctity of Human Life that is a start! But, encourage him not to stop there. That is just the beginning. Encourage him forward and pray for the spiritual strength and fortitude to do so in a way that pleases Christ.

VOTE FOR LIFE!

Many pastors find the simplest ground to speak out on the life issue, and that opportunity often arises in an election year. By all means we need to make the most of our freedom to vote. Each vote for a pro-life candidate or issue makes a vital statement to our country's leaders. Our church leaders should encourage us to vote responsibly when it comes to issues like abortion, however, if all your pastor discusses is how wrong abortion is, again, encourage him to learn about the whole picture. Encourage him to shed light on the entire "life" issue and to offer compassionate restoration to those that have been involved in an abortion.

As he begins to do so, a domino affect will start to ripple through your congregation. Sure, some will be angry and disagree. They may even leave the fellowship of your church. But for those that stay, they will begin to see one another more as Christ commanded. They will begin to be more vulnerable with each other. Relationships will deepen. Worship will reach new heights. An awareness of how dangerous sex outside marriage can be will begin to take root in your youth groups. This kind of awareness can bear an orchard of new fruit when given the opportunity to take root and grow.

BABY BOTTLES AND DIAPER DRIVES

Some evangelical churches have gotten involved in the life issue by supporting their local pregnancy care center. This is one of the most positive steps the church has taken. Most pregnancy centers are run primarily by volunteers. Their budgets are minimal but their impact is huge! These courageous people are on the front lines every day, ministering to the needs of women facing an unplanned or ill-timed pregnancy. They are doing what Christ called the body of believers to do, and they are doing it with limited resources. They desperately need the churches' support.

Beyond helping to save many babies through ministering to their mothers, more pregnancy centers are also successfully leading abortion recovery bible study support groups, reconciling these wounded individuals to Christ and restoring them to useful and productive service for His glory. While many of these centers are doing a fine job in this endeavor, I believe they should not be the only ones involved in abortion recovery. Christ said the church was for the spiritually sick. He didn't just mean those sick with "acceptable" sin diseases…He meant all sin!

THE OSTRICH SYNDROME

We, in the church, have buried our collective heads in the sand for far too long. When we have dealt with the life issue, we have focused almost singularly on saving the babies, neglecting almost entirely the needs of the parents. We need to get beyond merely bearing the physical, financial, and generic relationship burdens that are prevalent in our churches. We need to be willing to dig deeper into these issues and to accept that perhaps there is an abortion at the root of them. We need to remove the taboo label of abortion and talk about it openly based on truth, not the misconceptions or myths the "world" has led us to believe. And the place to begin is to ask God to enable us to see the hearts of those that have been wounded by abortion as He sees them.

> WE NEED TO GET BEYOND MERELY BEARING THE PHYSICAL, FINANCIAL, AND GENERIC RELATIONSHIP BURDENS THAT ARE PREVALENT IN OUR CHURCHES. WE NEED TO REMOVE THE TABOO LABEL FROM ABORTION.

CHAPTER 6

SEEING THE POST-ABORTIVE THROUGH GOD'S EYES

"I never knew people who had abortions suffered so. Honestly, I never considered how it affected them until now...."

– A Non-abortive woman

What We Don't Know <u>Can</u> Hurt Us

Several years ago a close friend of mine had a sore throat that just wouldn't go away. She had been examined by her doctor who had put her on antibiotics. She was on her second or third round of medication when a physician at church offered to take a look at her throat. He knew immediately something was amiss and recommended she see an ear, nose, and throat specialist.

What the first doctor didn't realize was that the irritation in my friend's throat was a very aggressive form of cancer. The antibiotics he prescribed were never going to heal her throat. In fact, had the accurate diagnosis been delayed any longer it might have been too late. What that doctor didn't know almost killed my friend.

What we in the church have believed about abortion all these years has been based on partial information at best and deceptions at worst. We have considered abortion as a political and social issue that is primarily about saving the babies and one that has little if anything to do with the people within our congregations. What we believed was a sore throat is really a deadly

> WHAT WE BELIEVE IS A SORE THROAT IS REALLY A DEADLY CANCER, AND IT IS DESTROYING THE LIVES OF MILLIONS OF CHRISTIANS IN THIS COUNTRY.

cancer, and it is destroying the lives of millions of Christians in this country. Further, many pastors and church leaders have counseled women and couples to abort, or supported their decision to abort in unfortunate situations and for "acceptable" reasons (e.g. fetal abnormalities or risk to the life of the mother). They have done so out of concern for these people, but also out of a lack of knowledge and understanding of the larger scope and impact of abortion. What we, as Christians, haven't known has hurt us. And it has hurt the people that have trusted us for wise counsel. [See Chart 6:1]

CHART 6:1 WHY ABORTION IS NEVER OKAY

- Abortion terminates the life of an unborn child.
- God is the Creator of life which makes every life valuable [Psalm 139:13-16; Jeremiah 1:5]
- God has commanded us not to take the life of another [Deuteronomy 5:17]
- God is sovereign;
  - Nothing escapes His notice [Hebrews 4:13; Psalm 139:1-4]
  - Nothing occurs without His permission [Job 1]
  - All events serve His will [Romans 8:28-29]
- He knew us and ordained all our days before we were born [Psalm 139:16]
- Abortion doesn't solve a problem, it creates a wound our souls were never meant to bear, which in turn causes many other problems: Abortion wounds every life it touches [Jeremiah 31:15]

We in the church haven't known, but now we do. We know that post-abortion trauma can be and often is so emotionally painful, the regret so great, that many times the abortion-affected person despairs to the point of taking his/her own life. Many of the people I have talked with over the years have considered suicide. A frightening number have threatened it or actually attempted it.

Many others behave so self-destructively that hospitalization is often required. Emotional breakdowns are common. Sometimes the only way they can handle the emotional pain is to make it physical through cutting or self-mutilation. This is also why eating disorders and chemical addictions are so prevalent within this population. Their pain is so great they try to numb it however they can. Sadly, when they sober up the pain is still there, only now they have another stronghold on top of the original wound.

Because their trust in mankind has been so violated (from influences pertaining to the initial decision to abort to the actual procedure at the clinic or hospital), they no longer trust other people. They close off their hearts to those close to them resulting in relationship problems on every front – at home, at work, with friends, family, and yes, even in the church. They are in extreme emotional pain and they feel entirely alone. They are convinced no one is trustworthy. No one can help. No one understands.

That is why we in the church *must* make an effort to understand. We must be aware of how abortion has hurt them and do whatever is within our power with the enabling of the Holy Spirit to create a safe environment within the church. We must get off our "righteous indignation" soap boxes. In fact, we must go so far as to kneel down and wash their emotional and spiritual feet. There is a reason Jesus modeled this action with His disciples. I think He must have had the abortion-affected in mind when He did it.

These wounded people need to know that we are here to serve them, to help them, to wash their wounds and to hold them when the rest of the world has so deceived, destroyed, and rejected them. They need to know that we can be trusted; trusted to love them, to understand them, to offer them the compassion and comfort from the God of all comfort. They need to know that there is hope for healing of this shattered place in their lives and that hope is Jesus Christ. We need to be Jesus to them. If we in the church aren't who will be?

"WHOM SHALL I SEND?"

In Isaiah 6 the prophet has a vision. Through this vision God commissions him to go forth on His behalf and on behalf of His people. The sin of the chosen race of Israel was great. They had offended God in the vilest ways. Yet His heart was still for them. His desire was for them to turn from their wickedness and return to Him.

> WE NEED TO BE JESUS TO THEM. IF WE IN THE CHURCH AREN'T WHO WILL BE?

God didn't treat their sin lightly. He spent the first five chapters of Isaiah describing their evil deeds. He had endured all He could; and by chapter 6 He has had enough. Yet it is not punishment He desires for His people, but reconciliation. After this tirade He asks, *"Whom shall I send, and who will go for Us?" (Isaiah 6:8)*

We can all agree that abortion is vile. It is wretched and evil. Sin always is. But, what we are talking about here is God's people. They have been lured away. They have been deceived. They have made the worst possible choices. Now they are wasting away in the aftermath of those choices. Who will speak God's heart of reconciliation over them?

CHAIN OF COMMAND?

The Word of God communicates two themes strongly and repeatedly through scripture that apply here: First, He places the greatest burden of responsibility for the flocks upon the shepherds; and second, while every church has a lead shepherd, none of us within the flock are without some responsibility.

Let me clarify.

It would be easy to put all the responsibility on the pastors and leader-ship teams of the church to take this message to the people. Ultimately the condition of the flock is their responsibility. However, those of us within the flock have also been called to bear one another's burdens. While the pastor needs to take the lead on this issue, it may be those of us in the flock that help to bring this issue to his attention and then support him as he goes forward with it.

Taking on the abortion issue as I've described it in this book is no easy task. Some people within the church will be upset that the "A" word is even spoken. Some will be angry enough to leave. And let's be honest; others may incite their peers to divide the church. All these things are possible. The bottom line is that we can do what the religious leaders in Jesus' parable of the Good Samaritan did [in Luke chapter 10]; we can move to the other side of the road and spout any number of excuses for not tending to the wounded people among us dying in their sin. Or we can be like Jesus and reject the excuses, be on guard against the "what if's" and minister to the abortion-wounded in our midst.

The truth of the matter is this: If God is moving in this country on behalf of the vast numbers of Christians and others that have been wounded by abortion – and all evidence supports this conclusion – then don't you think He will make a way even where there seems to be no way? Our God is not frightened by a chal-lenge. He knows the situation

> IF WE FOLLOW GOD IN THIS MINISTRY EFFORT, IF WE ALLOW HIM TO LEAD US, HE WILL PREPARE THE HEARTS OF THOSE AROUND US.

better than we do and He also knows that nothing is beyond His ability to achieve. If we follow God in this ministry effort, if we allow Him to lead us, He will prepare the hearts of those around us.

Will it be easy? No, you can be sure it won't. Will there be fierce opposition and spiritual warfare? Yes. Count on it. Will you say no to

God out of fear of difficulty, opposition, or spiritual attack? That, my friend, is between you and God.

If, however, you are willing to allow God to "send" you in this ministry effort to meet this hurting population at the point of their need and reconcile them to Christ, He will bless you and your church beyond all you could ask or imagine! That is the kind of God we serve.

WHAT NOW?

The first step in the process of tackling the abortion issue within your church is prayer. Bathe it in prayer. Seek God's face (and heart) on it. Whether you are the pastor of your church or the most insignificant member, pray. Ask God to guide your every step. Ask Him to give you His words as you speak to others about it. And ask Him to prepare the way.

After you've committed it to prayer, and as you continue praying, educate yourself on the issue of abortion. Learn all you can about the things we've discussed in this book – who has abortions, why they choose them, and how they are affected by them. (Don't miss the list of resources and recommended reading at the back of this book.) Isaiah 5:13 says, *"My people go into exile for their lack of knowledge."* And He echoes the same thought in Hosea 4:6, *"My people are destroyed for lack of knowledge."* Knowledge is power. Knowledge is key. Learn all you can as you continue committing it to prayer.

If you are a lay person in your church, talk about abortion with those around you from the perspective of truth and with great sensitivity and compassion. Share what you've learned with them. Help raise awareness within your congregation appropriately, as opportunities arise. One caution, however: Be ever mindful that there are many people around you that have been wounded by abortion. Choose your words carefully. Season them with compassion and understanding for the aborted person and be willing to defend them in the event you encounter a person that is embittered toward those that have chosen abortion.

Go to your pastor. Give him a copy of this book and ask him to seek God on this issue. Stress the importance of being Christ to those in the church that have been wounded by abortion and ask him to prayerfully read this book with an open heart and mind. Ask him to talk with you when he finishes reading it. Let him know that you support him and will be praying for him. Then do it.

If you are a pastor, you have the greatest position of influence in your church. The next step is to begin creating a safe atmosphere in your church. As with the lay person, educate yourself on this issue. Cover it in prayer and ask the Holy Spirit to guide you in preparing the hearts of those in your congregation to hear what needs to be shared with them. If you are willing, He will lead you and He will make straight the path before you.

As you begin talking to your congregation remember you have three very different groups of people in your audience. There are those that have been wounded by abortion and bear the burden of guilt, regret, shame, and condemnation. These are the ones that are suffering from Post-Abortion Syndrome. The second group is comprised of people that have been wounded by abortion and are embittered because of it. They are the grandparents or fathers that wanted the child to live but were powerless to prevent the abortion. Sometimes they are the mother herself if she was forced to have the abortion

> TALK ABOUT ABORTION WITH THOSE AROUND YOU FROM THE PERSPECTIVE OF TRUTH AND WITH GREAT SENSITIVITY AND COMPASSION. SHARE WHAT YOU'VE LEARNED. HELP RAISE AWARENESS.

against her will. The third group has never given abortion a second thought beyond the moral or legal perspectives of it.

Your challenge is to bring these three groups of people to the same point at the foot of the cross – the point of understanding, compassion, and a realization that all have sinned and fallen short of the glory of the Lord. All of us must give account for our actions and attitudes before Him. Begin treating abortion as any other sin and admonish your congregation to do the same. Jesus loved sinners. It was for sinners that He came to earth in human form – to tell them about the Father's love for them, to model that love for them, and to give His life as a ransom for their (our) sin. We must never forget where we ourselves came from, and each of us came from a life of sin.

> YOUR CHALLENGE IS TO BRING THE... PEOPLE TO THE SAME POINT AT THE FOOT OF THE CROSS — THE POINT OF UNDERSTAND-ING, COMPASSION, AND A REAL-IZATION THAT ALL HAVE SINNED AND FALLEN SHORT OF THE GLORY OF THE LORD.

Bring the sin of abortion into the light of the cross by the light of the Word of God. Show your congregation how Jesus defended the woman caught in adultery (John 8:1-11) – a sin punishable by death in those days. Show them how He defended her, shaming her accusers and saving her life before He ever confronted her sin. And even then He did not condemn her. He gave her life back to her and then He freed her with the admonition to go and sin no more. That is our model for dealing with the post-abortive…and how much more for the post-abortive Christians in our midst!

Once you have begun laying the groundwork within your congregation, the next step is to offer those people that have been wounded by abortion a safe, confidential place to share their pain and to walk through the healing process. Before you get to this point you will want to enlist the assistance of someone that has experience leading abortion recovery bible study support groups. See the resource list at the back of this book for suggestions.

The One that Sows in Tears, Reaps a Harvest of Joy [Psalm 126:5]

The result of your efforts on behalf of the abortion-affected will be a transformation in their lives as well as in your congregation. When we, as the body of Christ, are able to openly embrace those around us that have committed the sin of abortion, there will be few other sins that will remain under the stronghold

> WHEN THESE PEOPLE FIND HEALING IN CHRIST THEY BECOME POWERFUL SWORDS IN GOD'S HANDS.

and silence of shame. When these people find healing in Christ they become powerful swords in God's hands serving Him with a passion and depth of love that few of us can relate to. For him/her that has been forgiven much loves much. [Luke 7:47]

CHAPTER 7

MAKING THE CHURCH A SAFE PLACE FOR THE POST-ABORTIVE
HOW TO CULTIVATE COMPASSION FOR THE POST-ABORTIVE AMONG THE NON-ABORTIVE

"I knew God had forgiven me for having the abortion but I believed the sadness and torment I felt would be with me always."
– Stephanie

"It is said that if wombs had windows abortion would not exist. I believe that if the hearts of those wounded by abortion had windows, there would be no condemnation toward them in the church."
– Mary Comm

We've ascertained in earlier chapters that the church needs to establish itself as a safe environment for those that have been wounded by abortion to find love, acceptance, hope, and healing in Jesus Christ. What is it that makes a church safe for people to share their deepest hurts, especially when that hurt is a past abortion?

BREAKING THE SILENCE

The very fact that most churches are silent on the issue of abortion, with the rare exception of a passing mention on Sanctity of Human Life Sunday, is evidence to the individuals within those congregations that it is not safe for them to share their pain. For them, the silence is a deafening indictment against them. Were it not so, abortion would not be such a taboo word. The fact that few pastors will even speak it – much less speak about it with compassion and mercy – is all they need to continue keeping the suffering and shame silent.

SHUTTING DOWN CONDEMNATION

The first step is to educate those that have never been touched by an abortion – the non-abortive. This is why it is crucial that the pastor of your church is fully informed on the truth about who has abortions, why they choose abortion, and how it affects them. It is the pastor's job to level the field on the issue of sin and to tell the truth about abortion to the entire congregation as a step toward generating compassion for those hurting people.

Those that have never been touched by an abortion cannot be expected to understand the torment suffered in the hearts of those that have. Yet that understanding is vital if we are to eliminate judgmentalism in the church toward them. Since most post-abortive people are unable to speak for themselves publicly, it is the responsibility of those that do understand to speak for them. The understanding and truth come first, then the privilege and responsibility is ours to speak on their behalf until such time as they are able to speak for themselves.

When church members erroneously believe that women choose abortion, (a) because it is their legal and fundamental right to do so, (b) as a form of birth control, or (c) as a blatant act of selfishness, the result is often righteous anger and condemnation. However, when a truer picture is painted and people are able to see their motivations more clearly, and when the consequences of that choice are revealed, the result is understanding that leads to compassion.

Dr. David C. Reardon, well-known in pro-woman/pro-life circles is a biomedical ethicist and director of the Elliot Institute. Dr. Reardon has done many studies pertaining to the affects of abortion as well as statistics related to the post-abortion issue. In his book, *The Jericho Plan: Breaking Down the Walls Which Prevent Post-Abortion Healing,* Dr. Reardon offers a plea to pastors and ministers that are becoming aware of those that are suffering silently in their midst due to a past abortion:

"We are calling upon you, our clergy, to give entire sermons on the need for understanding and compassion for those who have had abortions. This can be done without in any way condoning abortion. Using as examples the testimonies of women who have chosen abortion, congregations can be reminded of how, in times of great stress, people do even those things which they most abhor. With examples of women who have been literally dragged to unwanted abortions, and those who simply gave in under the weight of many pressures, people should be helped to see that women are not always fully culpable. This does not lessen the seriousness of abortion, but it does lessen our tendency to judge and blame." [Page 15, The Jericho Plan]

Jesus said in John 8:32, *"you will know the truth, and the truth will set you free."* The truth of who has abortions, why they have them, and how they are affected by them will free God's people to embrace this wounded population with the love of Christ. It will free us to be His hands and feet toward them with the intent of reconciling them to Christ and restoring them to useful service for the kingdom of God.

SHARING HOPE

The second step in making the church a safe place for the post-abortive to share their pain is to speak directly to them of God's desire to forgive and restore them. Spelling out the character of God is key to helping them understand God's heart toward them. While God is a just and righteous God who hates sin, He is also the God who sent His Son to pay the price for our sins even while we were still sinners. Romans 5:8 clearly communicates this principle of God's character: *"But God demonstrates His own love toward us, in that while we were yet sinners, Christ died for us."* And 1 John 1:9 takes it a step farther: *"If we confess our sins, He is faithful and righteous to forgive us our sins and to cleanse us from all unrighteousness."* [Emphasis mine]

This verse specifies that there is no sin that God will not faithfully forgive when we agree with Him on the issue of our unrighteous deeds. Many post-abortive people feel their sin is too great for God to forgive. When they hear statements from the pulpit such as, "God loves you and forgives you no matter what your sin is…" their thought is, *But you don't know what I've done.* They need to hear – in clearly laid out terms – that God knows about their abortion and that His desire is to forgive them for the purpose of reconciling them to Himself. They need to hear that God sees their wounded heart and spirit and that His desire is to heal those broken places and to free them from the strongholds of shame and guilt. His desire is to give them the beauty of His grace and forgiveness in exchange for the ashes of their sin and shame. (Isaiah 61:3) Therein lies the hope they long for.

Speak God's passionate, lavish love over them. Use words that help them to see God's heart for them. Help them to understand that while He hates their sin, He loves *them.* As you do so, not only do you enable them to believe there is hope for them, but you also begin building a bridge of compassion uniting the non-abortive to those wounded by abortion. Offering healing words of God's love and forgiveness will set a tone of compassion within your church where condemnation once stood.

In the next chapter we'll look at the "innocent bystanders" of abortion and how to minister to their needs.

CHART 7:1 STEPS TO CREATE A SAFE ENVIRONMENT IN YOUR CHURCH FOR THE POST-ABORTIVE:

Step I: Speak to the Non-Abortive:
Educate and Encourage the Non-Abortive to Have Compassion Toward the Post-Abortive:

- Discuss and discount the myths we (Christians) have believed about abortion, who has them (statistics), why they choose abortion (deceptions), and how it hurts them (Post-Abortion Syndrome)

- Discuss Romans 3:23 and John 8:1-11, leveling the field, so-to-speak where sin is concerned and revealing God's heart toward sin and sinners

- Help the non-abortive to see the post-abortive through God's eyes; encourage compassion and understanding toward those that have been deceived into choosing abortion

- Caution them about expressing their lack of understanding, e.g. "I don't understand how anyone could abort their own child."

Step II: Speak to the Post-Abortive:
Communicate God's Love for and Desire to Heal the Post-Abortive:

- Reveal God's heart of compassion toward those caught in sin and His desire to set them free

- Let the post-abortive know God sees the depth of their pain and that no sin is beyond His ability or willingness to forgive, reconcile and restore for His glory

Step III: Invite a Healed Post-Abortive Woman or Man to Share Her/His Testimony:

- This step is crucial for both the non-abortive and the post-abortive. It allows both groups to see the heart of the abortion-affected in light of the mercy of God.

Step IV: Provide Trained Biblical Counselors for Those Needing Healing from a Past Abortion:

- Prior to Step 1 you will need to have some of your staff or church leaders trained in biblical counseling for the post-abortive (In Our Midst Ministries provides such training.)

- Invite those wounded by abortion to contact one of these trained individuals for confidential counseling

- Invite them to attend the 10-week post-abortion bible study support group in order to find healing and freedom (Flyers or brochures are available through In Our Midst for these No Greater Love support groups.)

CHART 7:2 TEN TIPS FOR CHURCHES TO REACH OUT TO THE POST-ABORTIVE IN OUR MIDST

To best minister to the needs of the post-abortive, you should:

- Know what leads an individual or a couple to choose abortion.
- Understand the societal and relational pressures to abort.
- Be aware of what post-abortion syndrome is and its affects.
- Be willing to exercise Christ-like compassion and acceptance toward the post-abortive.
- Set the stage in your church for loving and accepting the post-abortive.
- Receive specialized training in counseling and encouraging the post-abortive person in an effort to facilitate their healing in Christ.
- Volunteer as an intern with a qualified online post-abortion ministry. [e.g. SafeHaven Ministries, Inc. located at www.postabortionpain.com]
- Develop a plan to walk them through the healing process.
- Acquire specific post-abortion bible studies around which to build a post-abortion support group. [See resource list]
- Offer an open-door policy for anyone, Christian and non-Christian alike, who needs healing from post-abortion trauma.

Behold, I say to you, lift up your eyes and look on the fields, that they are white for harvest. – John 4:35b NASB

CHAPTER 8

WHEN THE TOUCH OF ABORTION EMBITTERS
UNDERSTANDING THOSE WOUNDED BY AN ABORTION THEY COULDN'T PREVENT

> *"Both my daughter and granddaughter have had abortions. They should be in jail for murder."*
> *– Anonymous Man*

INNOCENT BYSTANDERS...
When the Decision to Abort Was Not Their Choice

We have talked a lot over the past few chapters about how abortion doesn't just hurt the mother. We know now that abortion also hurts the father as well as everyone in the family, close friends, and those involved in the procedure at clinics and hospitals. While the mother's pain is unique and set apart from the wounds others experience, those others are no less significant.

What we haven't talked about is how those others are affected. As I've examined their stories, I've realized how widely varied the responses to abortion can be, even for those close to the abortive parents. For example, having been an accomplice, I experienced some of the same symptoms of post-abortion syndrome a post-abortive mother would. As a result, I have a great deal of compassion toward those that have made the choice to abort. However, those that were close to the mother, or those that became doctors and nurses to save lives, but were not allowed to be involved in the decision-making process often feel some very different emotions.

One gentleman we encountered recently was very bitter toward the post-abortive. He had lost both a grandchild and a great-grandchild to abortion. He was powerless to prevent his daughter and granddaughter from going through with their abortions. In the wake of the grief over those losses, his pain had turned to bitterness and contempt. There was no compassion in his voice as he expressed his outrage that they had committed what, to him, was an unthinkable crime. In his mind, not only had they committed a crime, but they had "gotten off Scott-free."

Another gentleman, a pastor I met a few years ago was in seminary when a fellow student and his wife found themselves facing an unexpected and ill-timed pregnancy just as this young man was preparing to enter the ministry. As desperately as this pastor tried to dissuade his friend from choosing abortion his arguments fell on deaf ears. This couple was afraid they wouldn't be able to follow God's call in the ministry with the added expenses of another child to feed and care for, so in essence they aborted their child for the sake of the ministry.

As I listened to this pastor retell his story, I was taken aback by his lack of compassion toward the post-abortive. Now, however, I understand more clearly where he was coming from. He was affected by that abortion, but not in a way that made him compassionate toward them. Instead of softening his heart toward the plight of the post-abortive, his heart was hardened, and understandably so.

If I had the opportunity to speak with this particular pastor again I would seek to minister to his woundedness where this abortion was concerned. I would pray for the Holy Spirit to speak words of truth to him,

> INSTEAD OF SOFTENING HIS HEART TOWARD THE PLIGHT OF THE POST-ABORTIVE, HIS HEART WAS HARDENED, AND UNDERSTANDABLY SO.

and I would validate his anger for their sinful decision. I would also pray that God would enable him to see how that abortion affected this couple. Are they still in the ministry? (I would be shocked if they were.) Are they even still married? (Again, upward of 80% of married couples divorce following an abortion.) I would pray for words of wisdom from God to shed light on the incredibly deep wounds the post-abortive experience; illuminating how it affects every area of their life; how it holds them captive in a prison of unimaginable guilt, regret, and shame... I would pray that God would soften his heart toward them.

If your pastor is reluctant to hear about the abortion-affected within your congregation, consider that perhaps he has been similarly wounded by an abortion. Or perhaps he recommended abortion to a woman he counseled years earlier. Even Dr. James Dobson fell into this trap. Believing he was helping a woman he drove her to a hospital for an abortion. Only afterward did he realize how wrong he had been. The guilt of a similar decision might well be weighing heavily on your pastor, either consciously or unconsciously. Rest assured, if he is reluctant to learn about these wounded people in his fold there is a reason. Pray for him and also ask God for wisdom about if or how to approach him on the topic. Whatever the case, follow the leading of the Holy Spirit in accordance with God's Word and you won't go wrong.

In this area of ministry you are going to encounter all kinds of people affected in all kinds of ways by abortion. When you meet someone that is hardened toward the post-abortive pray for and gently probe that person to discover why it is they feel as they do -- not in order to scold them for not being compassionate, but so that you can tend to their wounds as well.

> **ANYTIME SOMEONE CARRIES FEELINGS OF UNFORGIVENESS OR BITTERNESS TOWARD OTHERS, IT IS EVIDENCE OF A WOUND.**

Anytime someone carries feelings of unforgiveness or bitterness toward others, it is evidence of a wound. Ours is not to pick and choose to whom we would offer to be Christ's hands and feet and heart. Those embittered by an abortion they were unable to prevent deserve the same lovingkindness, compassion, and understanding we are so quick to offer to those to whom the choice belonged.

Bear one another's burdens, and thereby fulfill the law of Christ.
– Galatians 6:2

CHAPTER 9

SLOWING THE ONSLAUGHT/TURNING THE TIDE
THE HEALING CYCLE AND HOW IT REDUCES
THE INCIDENCE OF ABORTION IN AMERICA

"I am excited about allowing God to turn my misery into ministry!"
– A healed post-abortive woman

*"I tell you, her sins--and they are many--have been forgiven,
so she has shown me much love. But a person who is forgiven
little shows only little love."*
– Luke 7:47 NLT

THE KEY TO TURNING THE TIDE OF
ABORTION IN AMERICA

Many pro-life people in this country have devoted much time, effort, and energy to trying to pass legislation that will overturn Roe v. Wade making abortion illegal again. While this would be a tremendous achievement in many ways, and while it would significantly limit the number of abortions performed, it will not accomplish one of the most important aspects of the abortion debate: the changing of hearts.

God's Word says in 1 Samuel 16:7 that, *"The LORD does not look at the things man looks at. Man looks at the outward appearance, but the LORD looks at the heart."* It is the heart of man that matters most to God, and therefore it should matter most to us as well. So what will change pro-choice/pro-abortion hearts in America?

The answer to that question is both simple and logical. The pro-abortion side of this fight has been both crafty and cunning. They may "own" the secular media and a plethora of positive buzzwords, but what we have is the truth. We simply haven't applied it effectively yet! Over the years as I've witnessed the healing of post-abortive women I have noticed a fascinating phenomenon. As these women and men are healed through Christ, they respond in a variety of positive ways – all of which are effective in changing hearts in this country and around the world.

Some who've been healed through Christ begin sharing their story boldly with others, telling how their abortion(s) hurt them – which exposes the lie that says "abortion helps women." Others are so excited about this newfound freedom, forgiveness, and peace that they immediately want to help other victims of abortion find that same hope. As others accept God's forgiveness and their true identity in Christ, they are compelled to serve God and His people in numerous and powerful ways within their churches and communities. As people are healed, more people hear of the real story of the painfulness of abortion. The light of truth exposes the lies and more healing is perpetuated. The natural, organic growth of post-abortion healing multiplies exponentially; changing hearts (*healing* hearts) and turning the tide one ripple at a time.

> THE NATURAL, ORGANIC GROWTH OF POST-ABORTION HEALING MULTIPLIES; CHANGING HEARTS (HEALING HEARTS) AND TURNING THE TIDE ONE RIPPLE AT A TIME.

So what is the key to turning the tide? Very simply it is telling the truth within the church, loving and accepting this wounded population as Christ does, and helping them find healing through Christ so that they can join the chorus of truth tellers. Very simply, as more people tell the truth, more people will find healing, and more people will tell the truth, and more people will find healing....

FENCE-SITTERS AND TRUTH TELLERS

The apostles wrestled with a variety of issues in their service of Christ. To eat (meat) or not to eat. That was one question. At one time it had been a hard-line issue, but with the new covenant, Jesus ushered in grace, lifting the burden of some of those hard and fast rules. We might refer to that as a "gray area" in today's terminology.

Life is full of gray areas. Do we allow drums in our orchestra? Should we raise our hands in worship? What about the dress code for church attendance? Should women work outside the home? What about stay-at-home dads? Where should Christian kids go to school? There are no hard and fast rules for these issues. These are personal choices settled between the individual or family and God.

But as many gray areas as there are, there are as many black and white areas. Abortion is one of those black and white areas. God creates life. The decision to end a life should never be left to moms and dads. (We will leave the discussion of capital punishment for another time.) Abortion is not a topic for which we should fence-sit.

God values life because He creates life. His Word is clear that we should never take the life of another through murder. Is abortion murder? Not in the sense of hatred toward another

> IS ABORTION MURDER OR SUICIDE? SUICIDE: "THE ACT OF DOING SOMETHING THAT SEEMS CONTRARY TO YOUR OWN BEST INTERESTS AND LIKELY TO LEAD TO A DISASTER...[1]"

that leads to physical violence ending in death. I would refer more to it as a form of suicide. One definition of suicide is "the act of doing something that seems contrary to your own best interests and likely to lead to a disaster...[1]" Oddly enough this definition is the most fitting of all the terms pertaining to the ending of a life. Whatever we call it, it is sin and it is wrong.

Many pastors and church leaders will shy away from the abortion issue, choosing to fence-sit rather than risk offending some in their congregation. They will neglect those suffering in silence due to abortion out of a need to keep the peace or out of a fear of reprisal. Their fear is understandable, and I do not sit in judgment of them. In fact, I would go so far as to say that instead of judgment what they really need is information and education. With knowledge comes power. With understanding comes compassion. This is not to say that mere information will circumvent the anger and retaliation of some within the church. No matter how this subject is broached, there will be a cross-section of the church that will be furious that such a topic was discussed. In the final assessment, however, we are not called to be people pleasers. Galatians 1:10 says it best: *"For am I now seeking the favor of men, or of God? Or am I striving to please men? If I were still trying to please men, I would not be a bond-servant of Christ."*

Our example was Jesus, the Truth-Teller of all truth tellers. He was never a fence-sitter and neither should we be. Is telling the truth hard? Is it risky? Yes, Jesus was crucified for telling the truth. His apostles were martyred for telling the truth. Each of us that bears His name has also been called to lay down our lives for that same truth. In the final analysis the question is will you be Christ to those in your midst that are wounded by a past abortion at the risk of offending some in your church? Or will you cater to the loud-talkers and fence-sitters at the expense of the wounded?

Will you be a fence-sitter or a truth-teller? Will you help to turn the tide of abortion within your circle of influence, or will it turn you? Now that you know the truth about abortion, you have a choice to make.

1 *Encarta Dictionary: English (North America)*

CHAPTER 10

HOW TO BEGIN PREPARING FOR ABORTION RECOVERY IN YOUR CHURCH
LEARN THE TRUTH; SHARE THE TRUTH; PRAY FOR GOD'S FAVOR

"It is the highest calling and privilege to serve God; to be called His children and the ministers of His grace. The reward of the work we do is unparalleled, but if we're honest, so is the difficulty of it."

– Mary Comm

DEVELOPING A PLAN

Post-abortion trauma is a complex issue requiring a lengthy healing process in most cases. Because it is a post-traumatic stress disorder (PTSD) it is not something that can be mended with a "take two scriptures and call me in the morning" approach. The wounds from this kind of trauma, while deeply emotional and life altering are not outside our God's ability to heal them however, and we, as His hands and feet do not have to fear crossing into that territory.

As with any ministry effort, however, we do need to be equipped for the task at hand. Going into this type of ministry without sufficient planning and training can be risky – even dangerous, but with proper preparation, it can be an incredibly rewarding experience for you and for those you are committed to helping.

TRAINING

Because of the distinctively unique and deeply emotional wounds caused by abortion and the severity of some of the symptoms of post-abortion stress (PAS) specific training in post-abortion recovery is necessary. Obtaining adequate and appropriate training for this ministry is essential, but for those who have some counseling experience, a little education goes a long way. The foundational training can be obtained in a one- to two-day seminar, a service provided by a variety of reputable abortion recovery ministries around the country. [See list in the Appendix] We, at In Our Midst Ministries, Inc., offer trainings as well as ongoing consultations (free of charge) for general or specific questions you may have as you begin your ministry. We are here to equip you and to help you along the way as you grow your ministry to the abortion-affected.

ORGANIZING VOLUNTEERS

When setting up post-abortion bible study support groups, our recommendation is that no fewer than two facilitators (a leader and a co-leader) lead each group. These facilitators should be adequately trained not only in post-abortion recovery, but they should also have some experience leading small groups. Additionally, we recommend that the facilitators have some personal experience with abortion (either having had an abortion themselves or having been closely affected by someone else's abortion), and that each of them go through the bible study prior to leading the group. It is important to note that non-abortive people can effectively facilitate a recovery group, but they must have a compassionate, non-judgmental heart for those that have experienced an abortion.

PROMOTING YOUR MINISTRY

Within Your church...
Promotion for your abortion recovery ministry should begin in your own congregation, most effectively with your pastor or senior pastor. The pastor that has a compassionate heart for the post-abortive, that understands what

brings a woman to the point of obtaining an abortion, and realizes God's desire to heal and restore her can make the most effective inroads in your church for enabling those who have been wounded by abortion to reach out for help. A simple sermon (or sermon series) based on the grace and compassion of God toward the post-abortive can create a safe environment as well as communicate that it is indeed safe. If the safety factor is not there, if women (and men) do not sense that your church is a safe place in which to seek help, they will continue suffering in silence.

Another powerfully effective tool in creating and communicating the safety factor within your congregation is to provide the testimony of someone who has had an abortion, telling how that abortion affected their life and how they found healing through Jesus Christ. Nothing speaks louder than hearing someone say, *"I've been there... I know what you're going through... This is what helped me find healing and peace."* For your pastor to support this ministry by sharing his pulpit time to allow a healed and restored post-abortive woman to share her testimony speaks volumes.

Once the pastor has laid the groundwork and a testimony has been given, create a flyer describing your abortion recovery ministry – what its goal is, when the groups will begin, etc. – to be distributed in your Sunday bulletin for several weeks. Make sure you communicate that the groups will be meeting at an *undisclosed time and location* and that all participants can depend on *complete confidentiality*. This assurance is essential! (In Our Midst has a very effective flyer that can be personalized for your specific ministry, available upon request.)

If your church uses overhead PowerPoint slides, this is another effective way of reminding your congregation that this ministry is available to them. Run it regularly along with other reminders of church activities.

Another simple way of promoting your abortion recovery ministry is to put up posters around your facility publicizing the new groups. (We can also make suggestions regarding inexpensive resources for these.)

Within Your Community...

Networking with your local pregnancy care centers (PCC) can be an effective way of reaching out to those within your community who have been hurt by abortion. Many of the women who seek help from a PCC either have no church home or their church does not provide abortion recovery aid. Some PCC's do provide abortion recovery groups, so they may also be helpful to you as you begin your ministry.

Christian bookstores, small businesses, and some restaurants in your community may also permit you to display your abortion recovery posters or flyers. Your local newspaper may be a good place to advertise your ministry as well. Newspapers are usually on the lookout for opportunities to promote such activities that benefit the community. Local radio stations are another resource for publicity. They will often announce such programs by way of public service announcements free of charge.

An added incentive to publicizing your abortion recovery ministry within your community is that it becomes an effective outreach tool. It lets those in your area know your church cares about the deepest hurts people experience. This simple declaration will speak volumes to those wounded by other issues as well and they will be more likely to entrust their wounds to you.

Prepare for Spiritual Warfare!

Because post-abortion trauma is a powerful tool the enemy uses to deceive, defeat, and destroy the effectiveness of God's children, starting an abortion recovery ministry will be a declaration of war – spiritual war. Expect attacks from the enemy on multiple levels. Expect the attacks to be relentless. Realize and remember the enemy hates God and His children and he hates to lose his hold over them.

Remember also, however, that even though the enemy will be relentless in his pursuit of this ministry and those involved, our God is bigger, our God is stronger, and in effect, He has already won the war! The enemy has no power over us and can do nothing to us without first obtaining permission from our God. Each

> **YOUR ABORTION RECOVERY MINISTRY IS AN EFFECTIVE OUTREACH TOOL WITHIN THE COMMUNITY.**

participant in this ministry must put on the full armor of God and pray daily. Group facilitators should pray together regularly, especially before and after each group session. In addition, it is our strongest recommendation that you enlist the support of prayer warriors within your congregation to commit to praying for every aspect of this ministry including protection for your family members.

Pray

Our number one weapon of warfare is prayer, and according to the Word of God, we are to pray without ceasing. Do not be surprised either by the attacks that come or by the victory God delivers. The bottom line is that your abortion recovery ministry is *His* ministry, and it is His battle to fight. Your job is to remain close to Him every day in every way.

Abortion recovery ministry is a difficult road, but it is every bit as rewarding, if not more so! God is doing a mighty thing and if He has called you to join Him in this ministry, He will not abandon nor forsake you. In fact, He will bless you beyond all you could ask or imagine through your faithfulness to serve Him and His wounded children in this way.

"Be strong and courageous, do not be afraid or tremble at them, for the LORD your God is the one who goes with you He will not fail you or forsake you."

– Deuteronomy 31:6 [NASB]

WHEN THE BODY OF CHRIST IS WOUNDED: CREATED TO SOAR, CRIPPLED BY SHAME

For many women and men directly impacted by abortion the trauma has been immediate and overwhelming, causing a level of grief, guilt and regret that surpasses that of just about any other act known to mankind. What's more, many of them believe that because they knew it was wrong and did it anyway, it is a sin too big for God to forgive. Even if they can be convinced that it is not beyond God's ability or willingness to forgive, they are more often than not unable to forgive themselves or others involved in the decision to abort. The result is a large number of Christians are crippled by intense feelings of guilt, shame and unforgiveness. Who is walking through the healing process with them? Who is offering them the compassion and kindness of Christ without condemnation, without judging them? Who can they trust with such a heavy burden? Who is willing to bear that burden with them? The answer to all these questions should be their brothers and sisters in Christ.

Sadly, the church's long silence on this issue reinforces the belief that their sin is too big to be forgiven. What's more, when Christians respond to the topic of abortion with such comments as, "I just don't know how anyone could abort their own child..." the post-abortive are assured that non-abortive people cannot relate to them and therefore cannot help them. They are convinced the judgment they fear would be certain if anyone at the church were to learn of their sin. The result is that they keep their secret sin hidden and they continue carrying alone a burden the human heart was never intended to bear.

Christ died that we might live. He paid our sin debt that we might be free. He made a way for us to be new creatures in Him, more than conquerors. Through Him we have the ability to do "even greater things" than what He did when He walked the earth. That is our calling. That is what we were created for. Unfortunately, too many of God's people are bound up by the stronghold of condemnation brought about as the result of an unresolved abortion experience.

Our job as the church – the body of Christ – is to bear their burdens, to help them be reconciled to God, and to restore them gently so they can be

what He created them to be. That is what In Our Midst Ministries, Inc. is all about. Contact In Our Midst for more information, materials, and resources to help you answer the call to help those in your midst wounded by abortion to find hope and healing in Jesus Christ and to soar for God's glory. Call or email us today.

CONTACT INFORMATION:
In Our Midst Ministries, Inc.
P.O. Box 30621
Edmond, OK 73003
Phone: 405-330-0366
Web site: http://www.InOurMidst.com
E-mail: staff@inourmidst.com
In Our Midst Ministries, Inc. is a non-profit 501(c)-3 corporation.
All donations are tax deductible to the full extent of the law.

InOurMidst
MINISTRIES

APPENDIX

WHAT IS POST-ABORTION SYNDROME?

- Post-Abortion Syndrome (PAS) is a form of Post Traumatic Stress Disorder (PTSD).

- PTSD is the result of having suffered an event so stressful and so traumatic that the person is taken beyond his/her ability to cope in a normal manner.

- The events leading up to and including the abortion itself are often of such a traumatic nature that PTSD is often the result.

- Victims of PTSD or PAS are unable to simply resume their lives where they left off before the traumatic event. Instead they experience a variety of reactions that do not go away merely with the passage of time.

- Although the symptoms of PAS are varied, and although they may not surface for years after the trauma, they are nonetheless real and should be dealt with.

REASONS THEY ARE RELUCTANT TO SEEK HELP

- Intense feelings of shame
- Overwhelming guilt feelings
- Fear:
  - Fear of telling
  - Fear of rejection
  - Fear of being judged
  - Fear of condemnation
  - Fear of being exposed or gossiped about
- They don't want anyone to know what they've done

- They feel this sin is too big for God to forgive

- They have made peace with their abortion, having convinced themselves it was the right decision to make (This is a form of denial.)

- They haven't made the connection between their emotional pain and the abortion

- They believe those around them are not trustworthy

- They believe the church is not a safe place in which to share this pain

Because having had or having been involved in an abortion is a shame-based sin, the accompanying emotions are incredibly strong. It takes an enormous amount of courage for a post-abortive person to tell someone of their secret sin, and all the more when that other person is a Christian.

Even with all the recovery programs established within many evangelical churches in recent years, most churches still operate under the guise that "we are fine because we're Christians." Instead of functioning like a hospital emergency room (which would be more appropriate in many cases), the church continues to function (in many respects) more like a country club. People are ashamed of the condition of their lives, so they put on a happy face and pretend everything is okay for their brief time at church. It's no wonder then why few Christians share their abortion experiences with other Christians.

If the atmosphere in your church is one in which people are still reluctant to share a previous marriage (that ended in divorce) or other "more acceptable" issues, it is certain those with a past abortion will not feel safe to share their pain. Sadly, until they are able to share it with us, we cannot help them work through it in order to find healing in Christ.

RESOURCES

FOR FURTHER STUDY

Recommended Reading:

- *The Jericho Plan: Breaking Down the Walls Which Prevent Post-Abortion Healing* by David C. Reardon ISBN: 0964895757
- *Making Abortion Rare : A Healing Strategy for a Divided Nation* by David C Reardon ISBN: 0964895765
- *Aborted Women: Silent No More* by David C. Reardon ISBN: 0964895722
- *Help for the Post-abortion Woman* by Teri Reisser and Paul C. Reisser
- *A Solitary Sorrow* by Terri Reisser ISBN: 0877887748

FOR FURTHER TRAINING:

☐ **Piedmont Women's Center Training:**

Abortion Recovery Assistance
Embassy Suites Golf and Resort Conference Center
Greenville, South Carolina
November 8-11, 2006
http://www.piedmontwomenscenter.org/institute/

☐ **Heartbeat International**

665 E. Dublin-Granville Road, Suite 440
Columbus, OH 43229
Phone: (888) 550-7577 | Fax: (614) 885-8746
Email: support@heartbeatinternational.org
http://www.heartbeatinternational.org/training.htm

Heartbeat International's H.E.A.R.T. Training - "Healing the Effects of Abortion-Related Trauma" is a one-day training that will equip individuals in pregnancy resource centers, counseling agencies, or churches to effectively minister to those hurting from a past abortion/s. The consultant will address post-abortion stress in both men and women, tasks to healing, how to screen individuals interested in the program and go over the user friendly Leadership and Participant Manuals. Contact the Heartbeat office for more information, date selection, and cost.

☐ **Hope For The Heart Post-Abortion Leadership Training**

Hope For The Heart
12377 Merit Drive, Suite 300
Dallas, TX 75251
Phone: 1-800-488-HOPE (4637)

A comprehensive four-day training designed to prepare you to minister to women who have experienced the pain of abortion. Contact Kim Olson at Hope For The Heart for more information.

OTHER POST-ABORTION MINISTRIES AND RESOURCES:

☐ **SafeHaven Ministries, Inc.**

SafeHaven is a Christ-centered peer support web site where visitors can come to find hope and healing in Jesus Christ following an abortion, as well as what to expect when considering abortion. Information is provided about Post-Abortion Syndrome, what it is, and how and where to find healing from it. SafeHaven provides moderated 24-hour chat room discussions, moderated message boards, confidential email support, testimonials, trained moderators, and information and resources concerning post-abortion issues. Both men and women are welcome. SafeHaven is located at http://www.postabortionpain.com.

☐ Misty Mountain Family Counseling Center

Contact Greg Hasek
503.670.7277 or 503.684.6289
mistymtnfamily@yahoo.com
http://www.mistymtn.org

Misty Mountain Family Counseling Center specializes in working with individuals, couples, and families who have been affected by sex addiction, pornography and post-abortion issues for men and women. Misty Mountain is in the process of building a retreat center in Washington State where couples will work on healing together through structured programs and outdoor experiential activities. The focus will be on long term support for healing and restoration.

☐ Silent No More Campaign

Georgette Forney
412.749-0455
800.707-6635
Georgette@NOELforLife.org
405 Frederick Avenue
Sewickley, PA 15143

Janet Morana
Priests for Life
PO Box 141172
Staten Island, NY 10314
jmorana@priestsforlife.org

Silent No More Awareness is a Campaign whereby Christians make the public aware of the devastation abortion brings to women and men. The campaign seeks to expose and heal the secrecy and silence surrounding the emotional and physical pain of abortion.

• Educate the public that abortion is harmful emotionally, physically and spiritually with lasting consequences.

• Reach out to those hurting after their abortion and let them know help is available.

• Invite those who are ready to share their stories to join us in being silent no more.

☐ Care Net

109 Carpenter Drive, Suite 100
Sterling, Virginia 20164
Phone: 703.478.5661
Fax: 703.478.5668
info@care-net.org

• Care Net operates Option Line, a state of the art call center. Trained phone consultants are available 24/7 to help women in crisis and to connect them to their local pregnancy centers.

• Care Net promotes the Option Line through a multi-media advertising campaign that includes billboards, internet, television and yellow pages generating thousands of calls and emails every month.

• Care Net supports an affiliation network of 900 pregnancy centers with trainings, resources, and other expert help.

• Care Net seeks to plant new pregnancy centers in under served areas, especially in inner cities, where the abortion rate is highest.

• Care Net distributes over 1,000,000 bulletin inserts each year to promote the work of local pregnancy centers.

YOU CAN HELP TURN THE TIDE OF ABORTION

There are many ways in which you can play a part in God's work. You can talk to others about the truth of how abortion affects those it touches. You can share your abortion experience confidentially with a trustworthy pastor or church leader. You can pray for hearts and minds to be open to the truth about abortion. You can pray for churches to embrace and implement healthy abortion recovery programs as well as sexual purity programs (with the goal of education and prevention). You can pray for In Our Midst Ministries as well as other abortion recovery ministries. You can support your local pregnancy care center by donating your time or resources. You can support In Our Midst Ministries with your tax-deductible donations.

I have set up a website where you can learn more and become equipped to help those whose lives have been affected by an abortion. On the site, there is a place for you to share your thoughts, find out how you can become more actively involved, browse through our resource area and subscribe to our newsletter to receive the latest, up-to-date information. Go to your computer, turn it on and visit www.inourmidst.com for more information and resources.

"The Spirit of the Lord GOD is upon me,
Because the LORD has anointed me
To bring good news to the afflicted;
He has sent me to bind up the brokenhearted,
To proclaim liberty to captives
And freedom to prisoners;
To proclaim the favorable year of the LORD
And the day of vengeance of our God;
To comfort all who mourn,
To grant those who mourn in Zion,
Giving them a garland instead of ashes,
The oil of gladness instead of mourning,
The mantle of praise instead of a spirit of fainting
So they will be called oaks of righteousness,
The planting of the LORD, that He may be glorified.
Then **they will rebuild** *the ancient ruins,*
They will raise up *the former devastations;*
And **they will repair** *the ruined cities,*
The desolations of many generations."

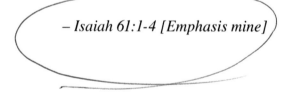

– Isaiah 61:1-4 [Emphasis mine]

Printed in the United States
72751LV00009BA/193-198